*To my dear friend Tanya,
The fighter for human justice,
with best wishes
John Ranz (author)*

Inhumanity

Death March to Buchenwald and The Last Jews of Bendzin

John Ranz
Prisoner #177243

AuthorHouse™
1663 Liberty Drive, Suite 200
Bloomington, IN 47403
www.authorhouse.com
Phone: 1-800-839-8640

This book is a work of non-fiction. Unless otherwise noted, the author and the publisher make no explicit guarantees as to the accuracy of the information contained in this book and in some cases, names of people and places have been altered to protect their privacy.
© 2007 John Ranz. All rights reserved.

No part of this book may be reproduced, stored in a retrieval system, or transmitted by any means without the written permission of the author.

First published by AuthorHouse 11/28/2007

ISBN: 978-1-4343-3671-2 (sc)

Library of Congress Control Number: 2007906849

Printed in the United States of America
Bloomington, Indiana

This book is printed on acid-free paper.

"What were the Nazi concentration camps? They could be compared to insane asylums. Except that the insane were not the inmates. They were the administration and the guards."

Erich Kastner, German-Jewish writer

The Author

Table Of Contents

DEATH MARCH TO BUCHENWALD

PREFACE   1

Chapter 1- Cobelwitz, Nitzah Arrives 3

Chapter 2- Searching for Partisans 7

Chapter 3- A New Lease on Life 10

Chapter 4 - Wachmeister Kopicky 13

Chapter 5 - The Auschwitz Universe 15

Chapter 6-Dr. Schmidt 20

Chapter 7- Blind Love or Suicidal Irresponsibility 23

Chapter 8- The Russian Front Nears............................. 25

Chapter 9-We Leave K-Z Blechhamer 29

Chapter 10-Passing Cobelwitz..................................... 33

Chapter 11-Rejoining the Main Marching Column............ 36

Chapter 12-K-Z Gross-Rosen 41

Chapter 13- Deeper into Germany 45

Chapter 14-Weimar 49

Chapter 15-K-Z Buchenwald, Human Solidarity in Hell 54

Chapter 16- Block 49, Walter from Saarbrucken 57

Chapter 17-Hunger.. 60

Chapter 18- The Underground- Political Prisoners............. 63

Chapter 19-The Last Desperate Agony and Liberation......... 68

Chapter 20-After Liberation... 75

Chapter 21- From Buchenwald into Southern Germany, My Unfortunate Brothers............................. 79

Chapter 22- The Children, Their Rescuers 85

Chapter 23- Conclusion.. 87

THE LAST JEWS OF BENDZIN: 1939-1944

PREFACE TO 1st EDITION 93
CHAPTER I- LIFE UNTIL 1939 94
CHAPTER II- THE FIRST PERIOD OF THE GERMAN REICH.. 97
The Nazis Are Coming 97
Confiscations and Extortions.. 99
Armbands and Law Enforcement 101
Going to Russia 101
The Kibbutz.. 103
CHAPTER III- THE SOCIAL AND POLITICAL LIFE OF THE TOWN'S YOUTH 106
The Factories 106
The Youth Groups and the Moazah 107
The Judenrat... 110
Schools.. 113

  The Press 115
  Libraries 115
  The Seminars 117
  The Slovakian Hope 118
  Ideological Regroupments 122
  Political Parties 125

CHAPTER IV- THE LAST PERIOD 127
  The First Mass Extermination 127
  In the Stadium 129
  Saving Lives 131
  The Problem of Self Defense 135
  The Story of the Partisans 138
  The Collaborators Disappear 143
  The Second Expulsion 145
  The Last Days of Bendzin 150

EPILOGUE 153

CHAPTER V- SILHOUETTES 154
  Baruch Gaftek 154
  Hershl Springer 155
  Hanka Borenstein 156
  Nadzia Klugman 157
  Israel Diamant 157
  Jacob Weizman 158
  The Pesachson Sisters 159
  Bobo Graubard 160
  Frumkah Plotnitzkah 161

Other Works by John Ranz

Tears on Tisha B'Av: Memoirs From the Holocaust.......... 165

Misconceptions and Truth About The Holocaust.............. 170

DEATH MARCH TO BUCHENWALD

PREFACE

I wish to dedicate these memoirs to my parents and my brother, Abramek, to my wife Nitzah's parents, her six brothers and sisters, as well as to our relatives, who numbered over one hundred. They were murdered by the Nazis, mainly in the Auschwitz extermination camp, and in the ghettoes of Poland.

Equally, I dedicate these pages to the memory of the millions, from all of Europe, of all religions and nationalities, Jews and Gentiles, who were victims of the curse of the twentieth century, Nazism, the most barbarous evil in the entire history of human civilization.

National Socialism, the German brand of fascism, was embraced by the German upper classes to rescue them from the deep economic crisis of the 1920s and 1930s. The purpose of this joint venture of German capitalism and fascism was to secure their privileged existence via expansion, first in Europe and then the world. The cost was millions of innocent lives, including one and a half million Jewish children.

The liberated prisoners of Buchenwald took this oath:

"We will dedicate the rest of our lives to the elimination of Nazism-Fascism and its roots from the face of the earth and to the establishment of a world based on human freedom and justice."

This oath should be adopted by the entire human race, now and forever.

I wish to thank Marie Shear for her help in editing the first part of this book.

Lastly I wish to express gratitude to my daughter, Shirley Ranz, without whom this book would never have come to be.

Chapter 1 - Cobelwitz, Nitzah Arrives

In the Spring of 1943, I was taken from the ghetto of Bendzin, Poland to a small forced labor camp in the village of Cobelwitz, Germany, which was located two or three miles from the city of Cosel. We were about thirty Jews from the cities of Bendzin and Sosnowitz. We prisoners worked at the brick factory and the adjoining lime quarry. A German army major, named Shirmer, owned the entire plant and the estate. He was on active duty at the Eastern front. Shirmer's manager, a fanatical Nazi, ran the estate with an iron hand and no heart. He made us work at the factory the entire day and then forced us to work in the fields in the evening. Here we worked next to Polish and German laborers, and were not so strictly guarded. Their sleeping quarters were outside of our barbed wire enclosed camp. The Polish workers were from the Carpathian Mountains and were called Gorale, meaning mountain folk.

At that time, some of us still had our civilian clothing, which we kept in the adjoining barn. A forced labor camp was not a concentration camp, but the work I did there was the hardest physical work I have ever had to do. It consisted of taking the bricks out of the kiln and throwing them onto shelves to dry. Often I had to work in the lime quarry, digging up lime for the bricks. Luckily I was able to procure some food on the side, as did our entire group. Near where we worked there were fields of sugar beets. At night, we helped ourselves to some of the beets, which we boiled for half the night into sugar syrup, to supplement our diet.

I had additional luck. A woman named Lena, of German-Silesian origin, worked next to me. Lena spoke Polish well, and she was friendly to me and to the others. She showed compassion for our misery. For a while, every day, she brought my co-worker and me a slice of bread with butter, or something else to eat. She knew well that Gentiles were forbidden to speak to Jews, let alone to give them food. Most of the other German women we worked with came from the same village as Lena, but they were cold and openly hostile. Lena was an exception. When I planned to escape, I asked her if she would let me hide in her house. She answered that she couldn't endanger the life of her family. I understood.

I sent a letter to my girlfriend, Nitzah Bilard. She was still in the ghetto of Bendzin, and I told her to leave it (a risky illegal act) and come to Cobelwitz. At the time, I felt strongly that the ghetto had no future and would eventually be liquidated, with the people sent to Auschwitz. Sadly, it was so. My plan was to hide her at Cobelwitz for a while until she could find employment in the neighboring town. I wrote such letters to other members of the Bendzin Youth movement, urging them to procure false papers as Catholics, flee the ghetto, and travel to Germany, where there was a better chance to find work and survive. In Poland it was dangerous for Jews, even with false papers, because of Polish anti-Semitism.

Nitzah left the ghetto of Bendzin the day before its final liquidation. She said goodbye to her parents, tore off the Jewish star on her coat, and took the train into Germany, with false identity papers. From then on she was no longer Nitzah Bilard. According to her false papers, her name was Jadwiga Wilczynska. She became a deeply religious Catholic girl, always wearing a cross around her neck. Her story was that she had lost her parents during the war and that an aunt had then brought her to Germany to look for work. During their trip to Germany, the story went, she and her aunt had lost each other, and now she found herself alone. Nitzah took the train to Cosel and from there walked the two miles to our camp in Cobelwitz.

Our forced labor camp was surrounded on all sides by barbed wire. Our living, dining, and kitchen areas were just one room, which originally had been part of the barn. The bedroom was separated from the main room. In the bedroom were over thirty bunk beds, triple-deckers. There was hardly any space to turn around. Our guard lived about twenty-five yards away in a separate house.

One Sunday afternoon, another inmate called me aside and excitedly told me that a Polish girl was outside the fence and was asking for me. He thought, perhaps, that she had a letter for me. I walked over, and to my amazement it was Nitzah. I immediately let her in through an opening in the barn. The barn was full of hay for the horses that Major Shirmer kept. I was terribly worried that a German neighbor or one of the Polish workers might see her. If she were detected, it would end in tragedy both for her and me. Luckily no one noticed her. From that day on, she lived secretly in the barn. After work I brought her food. We talked and racked our brains for ideas of what to do next. The camp elder, Mr. Schweitzer, was constantly pressuring me to get her to leave. He feared that if she were discovered and denounced to the Germans, then he, as the camp elder, would be severely punished. Each day he became more and more insistent. The other inmates felt the same way. They stopped talking to me, and I couldn't blame them. I understood their predicament.

On the sixth day, I approached Stashek, a young Pole, who sometimes worked next to me at the brick-cutting machine. I offered him a deal. I had a complete suit, the only one I owned, which was practically brand new. I would give it to him, and in exchange he would bring Nitzah to his parents' home, the mountain village of Stryszawa, to stay for several weeks. I told him she was a Catholic acquaintance of mine, from Warsaw, and that her parents had just died.

Stashek was seventeen years old, and had grown up in Stryszawa. His parents were very poor, as were all the mountain folk. He had never owned a decent piece of clothing. A real suit was a dream, especially now. During the war, it was almost impossible to get one, even for a German. Polish workers in Germany had dance halls, where they went on weekends to meet girls. Stashek never went to these social gatherings, although he very much wanted to, because he didn't have anything decent to wear.

When I made him the offer, his eyes sparkled with excitement, and I knew he would accept. We were the same height, and when he tried the suit on, it fit him perfectly. He caressed it and stared at his reflection in the mirror, his face beaming with joy. Several times he exclaimed, "Jesus-Maria, I would never recognize myself. What a dream come true!" Yet he still hesitated. Perhaps he suspected that Nitzah was Jewish. I improved the offer, adding a dress shirt with long sleeves. I had no opportunity to wear it anyway. Stashek could no longer resist, and he agreed to the conditions.

Free Polish workers could go home every second weekend. The next Saturday afternoon, Stashek walked towards the railroad station. Nitzah left the camp through the barn and followed Stashek at a distance of twenty to thirty yards. They waited till they reached the railroad station to join each other, so that no one from the village would see them walking together. The next day the camp elder felt relieved, and all the other inmates wished me luck. I knew that she would be safer up in the mountains than in any other place. She arrived safely, and in the letters she sent via Stashek, she wrote that she was earning her keep by knitting and sewing, and that bread was plentiful there. She wrote that Stashek's parents were nice, elderly people. The only thing that troubled her was that, when they quarreled, each one threatened to tell the Gestapo that the other was hiding a Jew.

After a couple of months, Nitzah again appeared at the camp fence. We let her in, and she told us that she could no longer stay in the mountains. The Germans had been combing the area in search of partisans and illegal inhabitants. Stashek's parents had become frightened and asked her to leave. We were back where we started.

Chapter 2 – Searching for Partisans

By this time our entire camp was aware of the fate of the Jews in the Zaglembie region in Poland. They had heard about the final days, the selections, the resistance, and the liquidation of the Bendzin ghetto. Even the Judenrat, who had cooperated with the Germans, were sent to Auschwitz and perished there. Only a few hundred people were sent to labor camps. The prisoners at my camp realized we would not see our relatives again. We also received information about the destruction of the Warsaw ghetto, despite the courageous uprising. We felt that our time would soon be up. But we still hoped that, in light of the tight labor situation, the Germans wouldn't kill all the prisoners. Mass murder seemed so senseless, yet all our information pointed to extermination at the Auschwitz-Birkenau gas chambers. I spoke to a man who had escaped from Belzec, another extermination camp. There the gassing took place in large trucks, when the exhaust pipes were turned into the cargo area, where the people were locked in. This fellow was happy to be in our camp. What he had witnessed at Belzec was hard to believe. He was reluctant to talk about it, because if the Germans learned that he had spoken, his life would be in danger.

After some deliberations, the majority of the Jewish prisoners decided that if we could establish some connection with the partisans in the forest, we would make a break to join them and take our chances fighting. An inmate from the city of Zarki told us that he had a contact with the

Polish underground. We asked Nitzah to go there and check it out. Nitzah agreed and left for Zarki with the name and address of the contact. She arrived at the home of the woman and identified herself. As soon as the women heard that it was a group of Jews who wanted to join the partisans, she cooled off and told Nitzah to leave. She urged her to leave immediately because "the Gestapo may discover your false papers." Nitzah tried to appeal to her Polish patriotism and sense of humanity, but this only angered the woman, and she threatened to denounce Nitzah to the Germans. In the meantime the next train back toward Cobelwitz wasn't leaving till the next morning, and Nitzah needed a place to stay overnight. Hanging around the railroad station was out of the question, because at night the Germans had more time to check and verify identification papers.

Nitzah knocked on doors and asked to be allowed to stay overnight. After many refusals, a Polish woman finally allowed her to sit on a chair until morning. When Nitzah returned to the camp and told of us of the "reception" she had encountered, we were heartbroken. Our dream was gone. We couldn't consider breaking out without some Polish help on the outside.

Four weeks prior to this, an inmate by the name of Weisman had escaped to his hometown of Sosnowitz, where he had a large number of Catholic friends. He was sure that he would find a place to hide among them. To our surprise, he returned a week later. His Polish "friends," one after another, had refused to help. He couldn't even get food to survive. Seeing no alternative, he returned to slavery after tasting a week of "freedom." He was lucky they had not denounced him to the Gestapo. The Gestapo paid an award for denouncing Jews, ranging from a small amount of money to five pounds of flour or ten pounds of sugar. Weisman had concluded that the chances of surviving on the outside, in that cold, hostile environment, were practically nil.

Inhumanity

*Nitzah Bilard at age 16, on left, with her sister, Sine Chaiah
1945*

The author several months after liberation, 1945

Chapter 3 - A New Lease on Life

After a few days of studying the torn newspapers used as toilet paper in the Aryan toilets, I saw in the Help Wanted ads, " Girl wanted to work in the house-good food." I thought Nitzah should answer the ad and see if the demand for identification papers was not too strict. The job turned out to be at the home of a butcher in Cosel. Nitzah went there the next morning and worked the whole day. At the end of the day, the butcher's wife told her that she was very satisfied with her work. She asked for Nitzah's papers so that she could register her with the labor department and with the local police authorities. This was what Nitzah feared most, since her papers were not good enough to withstand a thorough investigation. She told the butcher's wife that she had left her papers with some Polish friends and that she would return with them the next day. She walked back to the camp that evening, despondent. She very much wanted to stay at the butcher's, since it would mean plenty to eat, a normal bed, and an end to wandering from place to place.

After a couple of days, I found another ad, "Baker looking for a girl to do household work." We decided Nitzah should try again. The next morning she returned to Cosel and reported to the baker. At the end of the day, the baker's wife reported that she was very pleased with Nitzah's work. Besides cleaning, she tested Nitzah's skills in sewing, knitting, ironing, etc. The same scenario was repeated, with the baker's wife telling her to return the next day with her papers to be registered with the proper authorities. That evening, when Nitzah came back to the camp, we sat up till late, deliberating on what to do. Her identity papers were forged, and how would she be able to respond to the interrogation? There would be questions about the whereabouts of her family, her birth certificate, what church she attended, and many other questions for which she had no answer. Nevertheless, Nitzah decided to return to the baker the next morning and take her chances with a story that her parents had died during the war and that she had become separated from the aunt who had brought her into Germany. Asked where she had lived before she came to Germany, she gave the name of a Catholic family in Ostrov Masowiecki, the city she had grown up in. She knew that the city had been in Russian hands at the beginning of the war, and its records had probably been destroyed. Her papers stated that she was fourteen years old, making credible her claim that she could not remember her previous addresses.

I knew that the labor department could hardly be satisfied with her oral testimony and that it would seek verification from the authorities in Poland. On the other hand, I knew that there were millions of workers from the east, many of whom had improper identity papers or insufficient documentation due to bombed-out cities, burned-out villages, etc. Checking the papers of each young person was an impossible job. Besides, we figured that when they called her to a hearing at the labor department, if she saw it wasn't going well, she could always disappear again. Nitzah returned the next day to the baker to stay. She was assigned a room with two young German women. She was glad not to be with Polish women, who would probably have suspected her Jewishness. The process of verifying identification papers took several months, during which time she remained with the baker. She attended church regularly and always wore her cross prominently. Each morning she prayed in front of the crucifix hanging over her bed.

Two months later she was called to the labor department for a hearing. She was told that the Gestapo in the Ostrov Masowiecki area had been unable to verify the identity of a Jadwiga Wilczynska at the given address. Nitzah replied that her relatives had probably died or left the city.

The final decision was up to the mayor. Unbeknownst to these officials, she understood German. She heard the mayor saying, "Yes, the little one is perhaps right." The impatient baker had probably greased the palm of the labor official, which was common practice at the time, and Nitzah was approved. She was issued a regular labor book as the Polish Roman Catholic worker, Jadwiga Wilczynska.

As Nitzah later recalled, this was a fateful moment for her. It really meant a new lease on life. After that she destroyed the forged identification papers she had brought from Bendzin. She stared in disbelief at her shiny new labor book, with her photo in it. I was unaware of all this, as she had stopped coming to the camp for fear that she might be watched while they were investigating her forged papers. On a Sunday evening two months later, a girl dressed in a Hitler Youth jacket came close to the fence and asked for me. My friends immediately recognized her and let her in. She told me the whole story. She had borrowed the jacket from her German roommate in order to protect her from the Polish workers.

What most worried her was fear of speaking Yiddish in her sleep. She laughed as she told us that she had overheard the baker's wife telling her husband that Jadwiga's two roommates never went to church and that they must be descended from Jews. The German girls were simply too lazy to get up early Sunday mornings, the only day they could sleep late. Nitzah could not afford such a luxury and attended church regularly. She came to Cobelwitz again several times, even bringing some baked goods for us. I later discouraged these visits, sensing how dangerous they were.

Chapter 4 – Wachmeister Kopicky

Unusual experiences I had at Cobelwitz, occurred in late 1943, shortly before the camp was dissolved and we were transferred to Blechhamer. A new guard by the name of Wachmeister (Sergeant) Kopicky arrived from the nearby village of Bobrek, Germany. He was not in the SS, not a storm trooper. He was about fifty-five years old, a farmer and well read. He showed himself to be an opponent of Nazism. He tried to get us more food and to ease our hard working conditions. One day he came in and told us not to worry, that Hitler's days were numbered. Naturally at first we were afraid even to listen to such talk, thinking it might be a trap. Perhaps he was drunk. He did like to drink. We remained silent. Later his constant friendliness and decent human behavior convinced us that he was truly anti-Nazi. On evenings when we went to the fields to gather some beets and potatoes, he looked the other way, despite complaints from his superiors. He often shared his sandwich with those he thought needed it most.

One day, before Nitzah had gone to live with the baker, he came in to tell us that he had received information from the neighbors that women were visiting the camp. We trusted him enough that our camp elder, Mr. Schweitzer, decided to tell him the truth about Nitzah's visiting me and hiding in the barn. Sergeant Kopicky called me in to ask if it was true. Wasn't I afraid of the consequences if she were discovered by the Germans? I had no answer and remained silent. Finally I asked what he would do in my place. He didn't answer, scratched his head, and told me that she couldn't remain here. He then offered to take her to a camp of Jewish women. Nitzah rejected this idea. Then he offered to place her as a Polish worker on his sister's farm. A few days later, he informed me that it wasn't possible, since his sister didn't trust her husband, because "he was a real Nazi." Later, when Nitzah was working in Cosel, she sent me occasional letters through him. He delivered them to me but always asked me not to let her do it again.

One morning Sergeant Kopicky called me in a stern voice to report to his office, which was also his living quarters. Had I done something wrong? At that time I carried a first-aid box with me to work and I was recognized as a sort of medical assistant. With the help of medical books I had brought with me from Bendzin, I was able to order prescriptions from local pharmacies for some of the sick. Perhaps, I thought, I should not have done it without authorization. When I came into his office, he said that my girlfriend wanted to see me, and there was Nitzah in her Hitler Youth jacket. I asked her why she was doing this. She simply wanted to see me and thought it would be safer this way than to stand at the fence and be seen by the neighbors.

When the Cobelwitz camp was liquidated and we were transferred to concentration camp (K-Z) Blechhamer, he sent Nitzah a note telling her where I was. Sergeant Kopicky was a great human being, a rarity in a dehumanized German nation.

Chapter 5 -
The Auschwitz Universe

The concentration camp of Blechhamer was situated in a forest outside the village of Haydebreck, near the city of Cosel in Upper Silesia in Germany, close to the Polish border. Blechhamer was a satellite camp of Auschwitz, which was and probably will remain the most infamous place on the planet Earth. From 1940 to the end of 1944, the Nazis murdered about three and a half million people in the various extermination camps known as the Auschwitz-Birkenau complex.

Auschwitz, with its gas chambers located in Birkenau, had a ring of sub-camps around it, with regimes set up to cause faster or slower deaths. Some camps, such as Birkenau, were simply extermination camps where, upon arrival, people were immediately herded into the gas chambers. Others were hard-labor camps where people died of unbearable working conditions, starvation diets, brutal physical abuse, and lack of rest. In the labor camps, the Nazis did not kill you right away but used your labor as long as they needed it, or until your physical condition deteriorated to the point where you could no longer work. Then you were ready to be discarded and sent to the gas chambers at Birkenau.

I was prisoner #177243. This number was tattooed onto my left arm. The official name of the camp I was in was Blechhamer-Auschwitz #2. I had been transferred there from Cobelwitz, the forced labor camp, in 1943 together with a group of thirty Jewish slave laborers, who had worked in the factory and quarry making bricks for unlimited hours, with little food and no compensation.

The camp of Blechhamer, despite its electrified barbed wire fence, was not a "fast killing center." It existed to provide unskilled and skilled labor for a plant nearby that produced synthetic gasoline from coal. This plant was of the highest strategic importance to the Nazi military effort. It was a gigantic complex employing approximately forty thousand people. Except for the German civilian and military personnel, who were there mostly as supervisors, all of the others were slaves of different degrees. The slaves were of different nationalities and were treated in accordance with Nazi policy, which assigned each nationality a different place on the ladder of "racial" importance.

Western Europeans, such as the French, Italians, and Dutch, were treated better than those from Eastern Europe. Workers from the Slavic countries, such as Poles, Czechs, and Ukrainians, were close to the bottom. Below them were Soviet prisoners of war captured in battle by the German army. Except for the Soviet prisoners of war, most of the civilian workers could travel home periodically to see their families. On the bottom of the "racial" ladder were four thousand Jews, inmates of Blechhamer concentration camp. For us there were no rights at all, no norms of law governed us.

The camp was at the disposal of the plant seven days a week. Though owned and operated by I.G. Farben, it was ruled by the SS monsters. They could kill any of us whenever they wanted. They often killed prisoners for the slightest infraction, such as receiving a piece of bread from a non-Jew. Speaking to a non-Jew was strictly forbidden and was punished instantaneously by a beating that was usually fatal. If the SS guard did not kill the prisoner, he would report him for camp punishment - usually twenty-five to fifty lashes on bare skin, which few prisoners survived. The only contact permitted us was with our German supervisors.

The earliest inmates in the camp were Jews from the province of Zaglembie, in southwest Poland, also known as Polish Upper Silesia. This area embraced the cities of Bendzin, Sosnowitz, Katowitz, and smaller towns. In 1943 there had been an influx of Jews to Zaglembie from all over Europe. The last transports of Jews, who came in the summer of 1944, were from Hungary. The Hungarian Jews were first taken to Auschwitz where the "selection" took place. The Hungarians who came to Blechhamer were part of the "fortunate" 10 percent who were spared death in the gas chambers. They were young males, ranging in age from fifteen to the forties. They were in Birkenau long enough to witness the disappearance of their families into the gas chambers, and they described to us the smoke billowing out of the crematorium chimneys twenty-four hours a day.

Most of the work at the plant consisted of constructing railroad tracks, building roads, erecting buildings, or carrying heavy steel pipes and moving machinery to and from various locations. The Blechhamer plant was an ever-expanding colossus. Working mostly outdoors during the winter, without warm clothing, decimated the inmates. Our clothing was limited to striped uniforms made of a light synthetic material.

Only a small group had the good fortune to work indoors. They were artisans, such as electricians and locksmiths. Inside the plant buildings were gigantic turbines, hundreds of compressors of all sizes, and immense boilers that were five or six stories high. The entire plant resembled a refinery covered with miles of insulated pipes. It was under the management of the well-known Mannesman Company. Day after day, trains loaded to capacity with coal entered the plant and left empty. The Mannesman Company appeared to be the contractor for I.G. Farben, which was directing the plant and its production, and played a major role in constructing the Blechhamer synthetic fuel plant.

I was a slave at Mannesman. At first I worked as a locksmith and a blacksmith. I had learned these skills at a trade school in Lodz before the war. Our work detail was a little better than many of the others. We usually worked inside, under the direct supervision of German civilians or sometimes with French, Czech, or Ukrainian civilians. This provided opportunities to get an extra piece of bread or a part of their sandwiches. This was tremendously important to us since we were always hungry. At lunchtime we stared at the civilians as they gorged themselves on what appeared to us to be delicious, fantastic lunches. We had nothing and sat silently watching. Here and there one of them broke off a piece of bread and gave it to us. The prisoners who worked outside never had such opportunities. I once worked under the supervision of an elderly German, who hinted to me that he was a Social Democrat. From time to time he gave me part of his sandwich. Unfortunately my work with him was of short duration. He was transferred to another part of the plant, and in his place came a young Nazi, fresh from the Hitler Youth. Of all the non-Germans that I came in contact with in Blechhamer, the Czechs showed us the most compassion.

Our unfortunate brothers who worked outdoors were kept in closely guarded groups all day long. They had no contact with others. Their work consisted of transporting heavy steel rails on their shoulders, unloading cement bags from railroad cars, digging ditches for foundations, or just moving earth, sand, and rocks from one location to another. Their work was much harder than that of those who worked indoors. In addition they were exposed to the harshest cold weather in winter. How long people could survive under these conditions depended on whether they had a good kapo or a good guard. The latter was the deciding factor. Among the guards there was one, an elderly German, who looked away when a prisoner went inside for a while to warm up a little.

We left the camp daily for work at 6 A.M. and returned from the plant after dark. Every day, people dropped dead from exhaustion and starvation on the road to work or on the way back. Our food consisted of soup and a piece of bread that we received in the evening after we returned from work. This was supposed to last the entire next day. Most of us ate the bread at night and went hungry the following day. The soup was mostly liquid, lacking any fat or protein, which resulted in people's feet swelling up. Once we saw a person's legs swelling, we knew he or she was doomed.

Those of us who couldn't march anymore were assigned to the camp's infirmary, from where each week the sick were sent to Auschwitz for "Erhalung" or recovery, as the SS guards laughingly called it. Every day, people were missing from work, and we knew that we wouldn't see them again. Those who died at the camp were cremated. However most of the sick were sent to Auschwitz-Birkenau. In addition to the sick, the transports to Auschwitz were supplemented by the weekly selections. The SS guards picked out the old and the weak. These selections usually took place on Sundays, our only day of rest. In the morning we lined up for the roll call. Prisoners in each of the barracks, with its block elder, stood at attention. We were counted several times, and the Nazi camp commander or his assistant would review the lines and pick out the older and weaker-looking inmates, whom he claimed needed "Erhalung." His selection averaged twenty to forty prisoners, depending on his mood. The doomed prisoners were immediately registered and were later added to the transport to the main Auschwitz camp.

Chapter 6 – Dr. Schmidt

The clothing depot at Blechhamer, which we called Bekleidungs Kammer, was ruled by a vicious, bloodthirsty prisoner. He wore the green triangle identifying professional criminals and was a pure German, a real Aryan. Such people were a rarity in Blechhamer. I was told that he was in the camp for murder and rape. He had been transferred here from Auschwitz proper (Auschwitz I). Walter, the name we knew him by, was a real sadist and beat other inmates whenever he had the opportunity, often leaving his victims dead. Being a pure Aryan, he considered himself superior to everyone else. There was talk that even our senior camp elder, Demerer, who was nominally the highest prisoner official, feared him and was quietly avoiding him. Walter had excellent connections with the SS officials and always saluted them with "Heil Hitler." He may have been a former member of the SS. The clothing depot had several female employees, prisoners who had relatives or friends within the camp.

One night Walter came into our barracks shouting, "You international war mongers, you pieces of shit, I will teach you cursed Jews a lesson. Which one of you complained that your block elder is not distributing the food equally? In Auschwitz I would put this complainer through the chimney." No one moved. Then he asked, "Who is Dr. Schmidt?" It was obvious he knew whom he wanted. A man of medium height stepped forward and stated that he was Dr. Schmidt. "So you are the swine that made the complaint about your block elder, Mr. Spiegel, ha?"

Walter beat him brutally for several minutes until Dr Schmidt collapsed, unconscious. Before leaving, Walter warned us that this was a lesson to those who thought of complaining about their superiors. "I will send you all to the crematorium!" he shouted and left.

I barely knew Dr. Schmidt or anyone else in my barracks. My roommates were from half a dozen different countries. The "lesson" Walter had given left us in a depressed mood, but it was midnight and we fell asleep again. For several days I kept thinking about how we could get rid of this monster. The only way would be to get him in a tight spot and kill him. But then how many of us would the SS kill?

I later pieced together the following: Dr. Schmidt was a German Jew who had left for France shortly after Hitler came to power. He lived in Paris and was a dentist. During the Nazi occupation of France, he was deported with the non-French Jews. In Blechhamer he was assigned to our work detail, which consisted of skilled artisans, i.e., electricians, locksmiths, mechanics, etc. He must have had friends somewhere because he was given light work, such as cleaning our workshop.

Dr. Schmidt had noticed that our block elder, a Mr. Spiegel from Vienna, who distributed the soup each evening after we returned from work, was cheating us by doling out smaller portions than were available. After the distribution of the soup, he was left with a number of portions, which he gave to his cronies or traded for cigarettes and other food that had been brought in from the outside. Spiegel did no physically strenuous work since his duties were supervisory. He wore the best tailor-made uniform, which he had obtained by selling our food.

Dr. Schmidt, angered by the theft of the soup, had relayed this to a guard with whom he was on good terms, being a doctor and from Germany. With good intentions, the guard reported this to the roving SS guards who toured the plant and inspected our work details throughout the day. These were mostly young SS men, vicious animals. The one to whom the guard complained about the food "irregularities" had given Walter the task of teaching Dr. Schmidt a lesson, for prisoners were forbidden to discuss what went on inside the camp with the guards. Any conversation with guards or supervising civilians was strictly forbidden, except for taking work orders or asking questions relating to the work.

Chapter 7- Blind Love or Suicidal Irresponsibility

Both Nitzah's immature behavior and mine, motivated by our caring and love, could have ended in tragedy for us and for others after I was transferred to Blechhamer.

When there was no blacksmithing work there, I helped a young Czech to weld pipes. He and his Czech superiors didn't like the Nazis and behaved decently towards us. The Czech workers were completely free to come and go. This young Czech welder often warned me when he saw the roving SS guard, on a bicycle, overseeing the prisoners. Through him I wrote letters to Nitzah and received answers. Only later did I realize how incredibly naïve and dangerous this had been. But the worst of our irresponsibility was yet to come, an act that brought us to the brink of disaster.

With my encouragement, Nitzah decided to watch the prisoners marching back from work to the Blechhamer camp. On a Saturday afternoon, we marched from the plant toward Blechhamer. As we passed the Hydebreck railroad station, I saw Nitzah standing there on the sidewalk, among the German pedestrians. She was looking intently into the faces of the prisoners. The German pedestrians couldn't cross the street until the Judenlager, (Jewish camp inmates) as the Germans called us, passed. It was something unreal. I saw her only for a flash.

Death March To Buchenwald

She didn't recognize her youngest brother, Yosef, or me because we all looked alike, with our shaved heads and zebra-striped uniforms. I gave no signal or sound in her direction. It could have been deadly if I had. Blechhamer was not a labor camp but a concentration camp. SS guards, who watched our every movement, surrounded us. A simple gesture or surprised expression could have drawn the attention of an SS guard, which would have meant the end for her and me. Maintaining contact with the outside world was one of the biggest offenses, for which there was no mercy. I would have been hanged in public, in front of the entire camp, as a warning to others. I had witnessed this before at Blechhamer.

I was shattered by this experience. I could not have foreseen the troubles and dangers that followed Nitzah's appearance in the street. A number of inmates from Bendzin had recognized her and had traced her to her brother and me. For several weeks they visited me after work, wanting to know when I planned to escape and whether I could take one more with us. Others wanted me to send letters to their relatives in hiding. One inmate confided in me that his wife was in Switzerland and that, if I took him with us, I would be rewarded with a substantial sum of money. This was a disaster, because a camp informer could have denounced us easily for an extra plate of soup. This would doom Nitzah's brother as well. I now recognized the sheer folly of maintaining contact. Now I wanted her as far away from us as possible, so that she could survive and tell the world. We decided to break off our contact and leave our future to fate.

Chapter 8~
The Russian Front Nears

In January 1945, as the Russian army approached the Auschwitz-Birkenau complex, the Nazis decided to evacuate the prisoners and drag them deeper into central Germany. They hoped that the tide of the war would return in their favor, and that they would once again be able to use the prisoners' labor. By then I was already an "old-timer" in Blechhamer, having been there more than two years.

On Sunday morning, January 20, 1945, there were rumors that we would not be going to work the next day. The camp was in an uproar. People were telling each other strange stories. The night before, the prisoners of the concentration camp Jawarzno, another Auschwitz satellite, had arrived on foot. They had staggered into the camp, half dead. They were in a deplorable condition, most with frozen feet, ears, and noses, barely able to stand. They told us that they had been marching for several days without any food. Their camp had been evacuated because the Russians were approaching. Anyone who could not keep pace with the marchers was shot and left by the roadside.

I was standing near the gate when one of the columns marched in. I stood very close because I hoped to find someone I might know in it. I saw the kapos—prisoners picked by the SS to head a work gang or given other power, and their foremen swinging their sticks at the marchers to hurry them on, while screaming insults at them. They were trying to impress our SS guards with what good slave drivers they were, thus hoping to earn credit in their eyes.

We who stood on the side were overwhelmed with compassion for our poor miserable brothers. Whenever one of their kapos raised a stick to hit one of the marchers, we raised a howl of protest and even menaced the kapos themselves. This confused the kapos, and they stopped roughing up their prisoners. They looked around with perplexed expressions, as if to say, "What's going on here?" Soon our impulsive demonstration became dangerous, and our Jewish senior camp elder, or Juden Elter, chased us away fearing that the German guards might retaliate for our behavior.

The Juden Elter, Mr. Demerer, was by and large a decent fellow, considering the circumstances. He avoided physical punishment as much as possible. When the SS guards were in sight, he gave us tremendous tongue-lashings, calling us all kinds of names to show them what a strict leader he was.

Somehow he was able to save his wife and two children. He kept her in the women's part of the camp. His son was ten years old and was probably the youngest inmate in the camp. Demerer had immigrated to Austria from Sosnowitz before the war and had an excellent command of the German language, or so it seemed to me then. The older inmates, who had known him longer, had a rather good opinion of him. This was very important since it set the tone for the behavior of the rest of the senior and junior supervisors within the camp and reduced the brutality among the prisoners.

By Sunday evening, rumors were circulating throughout the camp that we too would be evacuated and would be marching behind the recent arrivals from the camp of Jawarzno. Next morning, the usual siren woke us up to work, but instead we were told to prepare for the possibility of being evacuated deeper into Germany. This was followed by another rumor that we were to remain after all. Due to the conflicting nature of these rumors, I decided to wait and see what would happen. I knew that a lot depended on what the plant directors would decide to do. If the plant stopped working, then obviously the Russians were close and we would either be evacuated or killed. I looked around and saw preparations to leave being made by people who had "connections." They were equipping themselves with clothing, which I reasoned they could only have gotten from the clothing depot. Walter, who ran it, must have known that we were to leave Blechhamer, since he started to distribute clothing to his non-Jewish friends and to the junior and senior camp inmate officials.

As the preparations to evacuate involved more and more people, camp discipline broke down. When I approached the food depot, I recognized people with connections to the food depot workers carrying loaves of bread and other foodstuffs. As I started to think how I could get some of this food, I saw more and more prisoners hanging around to watch what was happening. The mass of people now began to press forward and ask that they be given bread. The prisoner elders and kapos could not withstand the pressure of this mass of people, and finally the hungry crowd surged into the food depot. Many grabbed a loaf of bread and ran back to their barracks to eat it. The kapos were simply overwhelmed and were shoved aside despite their swinging clubs. SS guards arrived and started to shoot into the crowd. The mass withdrew somewhat. In the meantime, those hungry prisoners from Jawarzno, who had arrived the day before and for whom no food had been provided, were disrupting the normal food distribution to the barracks. These people were so desperate that they were ready to risk being killed for a piece of bread.

Soon a crowd formed again at the food depot, and inmates began grabbing whatever they could. I withdrew and ran to the clothing depot, where chaos also reigned. I could hardly believe what I saw. Waves of inmates, having smashed windows and broken down the doors, were inside putting on sweaters and underwear beneath their striped uniforms. It was an incredible sight, because in normal times these people would have been hanged or shot on the spot. The SS guards were not around in force. Apparently they were too busy making their own preparations for the evacuation and did not care what went on inside the camp.

At 11 A.M. we received the official order from the camp commandant on the loudspeaker: The entire camp was to be evacuated, and everyone should get ready. Since there had been no food distribution to my barracks and I was hungry, I returned to the food depot. I joined the surging crowd to get inside, grabbed whatever I could, and ran. Somehow I had gotten hold of two cans of meat. On the way out, I received some blows to the head from the clubs of the kapos. But I had a treasure. Each can weighed a kilo. These two cans kept me from starvation during the next two weeks of the evacuation march. After I secured the cans of meat, I ran to the bread depot, but it was too late. It had been emptied. All I found were the bodies of those killed by the SS guards.

Around noon, the order came to leave the camp. The roll call SS guard, who seemed to be the assistant camp commander, entered the camp surrounded by soldiers armed with machine guns. He ordered us to line up at the gate and then march out of the camp. He warned that anyone remaining in the barracks would be shot on the spot. Only the sick in the infirmary would be allowed to stay, with one doctor and a nurse. A sizeable number of those who had arrived the day before, some with frozen legs and in very weak condition, remained. Although they risked being shot, they felt unable to march.

Chapter 9~
We Leave K-Z Blechhamer

At noon the entire camp stood at the gates. The usual coterie of guards surrounded us, but this time they carried heavy, stuffed knapsacks in addition to their weapons. Their luggage was loaded onto sleds drawn by human horses, the prisoners. Heading the column were the women prisoners. At the end was a group of guards, fortified with additional SS men.

It was snowing, and we walked at a normal pace for the first few hours. We felt reasonably at ease. That afternoon we had our first death. After a few kilometers a prisoner, unable to march any longer, asked to be allowed to rest for a while. The guard took him into the woods and shot him. After an hour we met the French prisoners of war who worked in Blechhamer, and they told us that they had been ordered to return to Blechhamer because the roads were clogged with retreating German army units. It seemed to them that the Russians were ahead of us. This was encouraging news, but it proved to be overly optimistic. The camp commandant made us use the back roads, which added many additional kilometers to our route. We tried to figure out why he did this, and we came to the conclusion that our visibly deplorable conditions and the two hundred women with us might evoke some sympathy among the local population. He knew that the shooting of those who could no longer march would be witnessed by the German civilians, many of who were retreating, fearing the Russians. Perhaps he thought that it would be easier to find overnight shelter on the back roads.

That evening we arrived at the village of Reigersfeld, about eight kilometers from our point of departure. By then it was dark, and we were placed in a few large barns. Although I was tired, I couldn't sleep. The barn was so crowded that there was barely space to sit or stretch out. In the morning I noticed that some of the prisoners could not get up. Some of those around me decided not to continue and to hide in the area. They didn't believe that they could survive a few more nights like this. At that time, we didn't imagine that conditions would become much worse later on or that human beings could withstand such intense hunger and cold.

The guard blew his whistle and ordered us to line up in rows of five and to begin marching. The direction now seemed to be back toward Blechhamer and this cheered us. We took a shortcut through the forest, which was lined with antiaircraft batteries. Suddenly we stopped, and word went around that the commandant had met another Nazi official who told him that it was impossible to return to Blechhamer and that even the German air defense emplacements had received an order to evacuate. After a few hours of waiting in the woods, we reversed direction again and headed away from Blechhamer and deeper into Germany.

While waiting in the forest for the Nazis to decide, I was overwhelmed by frightening thoughts. Couldn't the Nazis shoot us all right there, by simply opening fire? Perhaps not, because many of us could run and escape. Why the long wait here? It seemed that the Oberstrumbahnfuhrer, the rank of our camp commandant, did not have orders about what to do with us. Word made its way back from the front of the line that he now had orders to bring us to the concentration camp of Gross-Rosen. This camp was situated in the Sudetenland, an area of Czechoslovakia populated by ethnic Germans, which in 1938 had opted to join with Germany. It was this area that Neville Chamberlain had yielded to Germany in an effort to appease Hitler at the infamous Munich conference. Chamberlain had assured the world that, by this act, he had attained peace and that Hitler had no more territorial claims in Europe.

Inhumanity

We continued our march toward Gross-Rosen. On the road we again met French and English prisoners of war and small German military units retreating in haste. We also saw German farmers and other civilians on trucks, horses, and wagons clogging the roads. Looking at the German military units retreating almost in panic, I thought of the "Siegreicher Ruczug," the victorious withdrawal. This was the term the Nazis constantly used in their newspapers after their defeat at Stalingrad. I was an avid reader of the German newspapers, despite the fact that it was strictly forbidden. I had had a special way of obtaining them at the plant in Blechhamer. Since the German and foreign workers lacked toilet paper, they used newspapers cut into strips and hung them on the wall in their toilets. These toilets, naturally, were only for Aryans. The prisoners had their own primitive latrines. I often took a risk and slipped into the Aryan toilets to take the "toilet paper." In the evenings, in the barracks, I put the pieces together and read them in order to know what was happening in the outside world, and especially to know where the German lines were. Together with the "victorious withdrawals," the newspapers constantly stressed the terrible fate the Russian army would encounter as it made its way further into Germany. The reader was supposed to believe that the Fuhrer was intentionally luring the Russians deeper into the Reich, in order to encircle and completely destroy them.

As we marched I heard the military shouting, "All those with machine guns (Panzer Faust unit) report immediately to the front". This also gave me the impression that Russian tanks could not be too far away. The Panzer-Faust was regarded as Germany's great hope to stop the Russian tanks. The German newspapers were full of descriptions of heroic soldiers who had single handedly knocked out dozens of Russian tanks.

Hearing these orders, we became hopeful. Somehow the march slowed down. We also noticed that some of our guards, particularly the older ones, had disappeared, and the others seemed confused. As we got closer to the city of Cosel we crossed a bridge. The bridge guards told us that the main column from our camp had crossed it more than an hour ago. This meant that we were separated from the main column. As soon

Death March To Buchenwald

as we crossed the bridge, we heard it being blown up behind us. From this we concluded that the Russians must be close. Around 11P.M. we stopped at a village and were squeezed into several barns. Our group, which was separated from the main column, consisted of approximately four hundred men and a few women. Looking around, I noticed only about a dozen guards. Among them was a brutal ethnic German from Romania who kicked and beat prisoners at the slightest provocation. He participated in the killing of those who could no longer walk and left their bodies in the snow at the side of the road.

Chapter 10 - Passing Cobelwitz

As we passed through the village of Cobelwitz, my experiences there suddenly came back to me. A few of the inmates with whom I marched remembered the village and "the good old days" we had there. We remembered Sergeant Kopicky, whom we called an angel, such a good German. We recalled the boiling of potatoes and sugar beets late into the night. I strained my eyes to see if I could find someone in the village that I knew, but in vain. I saw only stern-looking faces of people unknown to me, perhaps village guards. I was so aroused emotionally that I suddenly decided to escape from the marching prisoners. While a guard looked away, I slipped into a farmer's home near the road. Inside was a woman of about fifty and her twenty year-old daughter. They gave me something to eat and in addition prepared a package of food. They agreed to let me hide in their barn. However, I gave up this idea because I felt I simply could not trust them, and that, at their first opportunity, they would report me and I would be shot.

They treated me well, perhaps out of fear, because they had no male protector in the house, and I must have looked intimidating. I was in a prisoner's uniform, unshaven for days, covered in a blanket-a wild man. After I ate I decided to rejoin the marchers, who had already passed the village. While hurrying to join the marchers, I passed a number of dead bodies lying in the snow, shot and kicked aside by the road. They were all in the striped uniforms of the concentration camps.

Suddenly a voice called out to me. I looked around and saw an inmate from my barracks at Blechhamer. He was sitting by the side of the road, still alive but unable to walk. I knew that if I left him there he would be killed within the hour. Somehow the rear guards of our camp had not noticed him. I tried to help him to walk, and gave him some food, but it was no use. The poor man couldn't stand on his feet, and when I lifted him up he collapsed again. As I struggled to help him up once more, I saw a young village guard, about seventeen years old, coming toward me with a menacing expression. I tried to explain to him, in local dialect, that we were trying to join the camp marchers. This prisoner was having a little difficulty, I lied, and I had been assigned to help him. The guard didn't want to listen. He pointed his rifle at me and screamed, "March or I will shoot!" I had to abandon the poor man and run. After I had covered about fifty yards, I heard two shots. I knew that the inmate was finished. In my mind I saw him rolling down the road into the gutter, with the young murderer standing over him. I moved faster, fearing that the guard, a member of the Volksturm, might now take aim at me. It was already dark, and I soon caught up with the marchers. The SS guards didn't see where I had come from, so I got away with just a few kicks from their boots. I disappeared fast into the mass of marchers.

Once inside the marching column, I began to think again of a way to escape. I came to the conclusion that it wouldn't work, since there was no place to hide. Most of the people in the area were hostile, hating us because Hitler said to. They were mostly Nazis and hoped for a German victory. At work, in conversation with some of these Germans, they would tell me,

"You Jews are condemned to work for us as long as you live. You can never get married or have children, and when the war is over you will stay in isolation forever. Should we lose the war, you will all be shot before the end."

That was the official line of the Germans at the plant. It was depressing for us to hear their plans for us. The German workers all believed in the Wunder Waffe, a miracle weapon that the Fuhrer would be announcing any day. Their belief in this weapon kept them from collapsing spiritually, since they were aware of the constant retreats and defeats.

We passed Cobelwitz and came close to Cosel, where the guards found a barn for our overnight stay. After an entire day of walking in the snow, we were dead tired and stretched out on the floor. The next morning we continued marching. I was assigned to a group that pulled the sleds, carrying the belongings of the guards. At the end of the day, we arrived at the city of Oberglogau and were quartered in an empty sugar mill. There was some heating available, and for the first time some prisoners took off their shoes. This was a dangerous thing to do, often resulting in tragedy. It felt better momentarily, but in the morning the prisoners were unable to put the shoes back on, because their feet were so swollen. In order to put the shoes on, they sometimes had to cut them. Then they realized that their fate was sealed, for how could they march in the snow with shoes cut open?

We remained in this city the entire day. The next day we were to join up with the main column of marchers from Blechhamer. During our stay in Oberglogau, some prisoners sneaked away to visit houses in the area, in hopes of getting food from the local Germans. Some of us were even able to get hot food. Generally German civilians in Oberglogau did not refuse a piece of bread, if you were able to reach their house. Not many of us could do this. This was not a bad "stop" as we called it. In terms of food, many of us were able to improve our situation, but it was the last "good" day of the entire evacuation.

Chapter 11 - Rejoining the Main Marching Column

The next afternoon, at about 2P.M., we rejoined the main group from our camp. We immediately noticed a different situation. The guards were more hostile and more numerous. We learned that these prisoners had not eaten for several days. Today they had finally received eight ounces of bread per person. They were famished and much weaker than those in our group. Seeing this, we gave our friends and acquaintances most of the supplies we had with us.

During our overnight stays in the barns, I had filled my pockets with wheat kernels. Some of the prisoners had refused to do this, believing that the kernels could not be digested. I ate these kernels all day long, just to have something in my mouth. Little did I know what good nutritional value these kernels had. Sometimes they were all I ate the entire day. Our friends from the main marching column told us that they had been searching in garbage cans and would eat what food they could find there. They had eaten the bread distributed at Blechhamer on the first day, and this was now the eighth day of the march. In my knapsack I had some sugar, which I had found in the sugar mill the night before. I gave it all to my friends, who were clearly in a much worse condition than I. Here, in the main column, the guards were shooting prisoners for leaning out of the line or were beating them with their rifle butts. Prisoners were risking their lives, running into roadside houses to beg for bread. Here and there a farmer gave away a few potatoes.

Seeing the dead bodies of the prisoners on the roadside was very depressing. It clearly showed what my fate would be were I not able to continue walking. There was no shortage of the sick and elderly, and it was impossible to know how many were being killed daily at the rear of the column. That night we came again to a farm and were squeezed into a barn. There was almost no place to lie down. The last people to enter had to sleep on the floor. During the night, we could hear the screams of prisoners who were being robbed of their food by other prisoners. The victims were mostly the elderly and the weak, who had no friends to help them. The guards didn't care if the food distribution was orderly or equal. Often the weak got nothing, and the kapos got a double portion.

One of my friends told me that he had no sensation in his feet. He thought they were frozen. I immediately helped him remove his shoes and saw his feet were stiff, like ice. I massaged his feet half the night with all my strength, until at last the blood began to circulate again and the stiffness went away. I was very careful every evening, as we came into the barn, to remove my shoes, massage my feet, and then wrap my blanket or rags around them. I urged my neighbors to do the same. I also advised my friends, that despite their fatigue, to climb to the highest spot in the barn, since it was the warmest and safest area.

Running out of the line to the roadside houses, or stopping to rest, was risking one's life. Sometimes, a good guard quietly tolerated it. Other guards would shoot to kill. Either way, it had to be done fast, very fast. I once jumped out of the line with a friend, into a house. The people were sitting around a table, eating dinner. In the center of the table stood a large pot of boiled potatoes. Nearby were bowls of vegetables and a smaller pot of meat. There was no time to implore with words. My friend grabbed the pot with the potatoes and ran back into the marching column. The farmer, astounded by our action, came out laughing. We had often grabbed potatoes from pigpens. We had to mingle with the marchers and in a few minutes the pot had been emptied and was left by the roadside.

These desperate measures sometimes ended badly. If you fell when a guard caught you and hit you with his rifle butt, he would often finish you off with the butt or a bullet. As darkness fell, we took more chances, but the guards increased their shooting.

For a while, I marched in the very rear and observed the fate of those unable to walk. Some guards did not want to shoot these unfortunate prisoners, who had stopped or sat down in the snow. They joked to each other, "Let him sleep, let him rest." They knew very well that within an hour the poor soul would be frozen or killed by a bullet from the local village Volksturm or the SS guard who followed. I saw prisoners take away the blankets of those who stopped walking; justifying it by saying the prisoners would not need them anymore. Such cases did not happen often.

Frequently I saw that in the morning not everyone came out of the barn. Those who remained inside felt that they couldn't continue and did not wish to die on the road. Some hoped to survive by remaining hidden in the hay. Perhaps the Russians would arrive before they died. They couldn't reason. They only knew that they couldn't march any longer. The farmers who found them in the barn would call the police. Depending on the local police chief, they would either be shot or transported to the marching prisoners.

I had seen local police bringing groups of those who remained in the barns. Even a small rest for a day or two could sometime save their lives. Eventually all those who hid in the barns were discovered. They had to come out because of hunger. Each day more and more were dropping out of the march because of starvation and inability to walk. The rest of us motivated ourselves to continue by thinking that our destination, Gross-Rosen, was not very far.

By now we had passed the city of Schweidnitz, in the Sudetenland. How much longer must we suffer before we could be in a camp again, with at least a daily portion of bread? The night before, a bitter cold wind blew in our faces as we walked in the very deep snow. The pace became very slow, and it dragged on and on. Would it ever end? Around 11P.M. an order came to turn around. We had been marching in the wrong direction. Two hours later we arrived at a village and were squeezed into a barn. Even the guards were angry about having to march so late into the night. They vented their anger at the prisoners, beating them even more than usual.

Most of the guards were brutal sadists. They often teased us with, "So, you didn't get your bread today" or "Stop marching and take a rest." The guards had plenty of food, which they brought from the farms in packages whenever we stopped for a while. The only prisoners who ever got a piece of bread from them were the ones who pulled the sleds carrying their belongings. I wondered how long we could stand this life. I was losing hope that many of would survive if these conditions lasted much longer - the bitter cold, wet feet, and cold nights in the barns with very little sleep or food.

Two weeks had passed since we left Blechhamer, which by now we were referring to as "golden Blechhamer." We remarked to each other that it hadn't been so bad there. After all, we had had a straw bed to lie down on, with two blankets. Each morning there was a portion of bread and each evening some warm soup. What warm soup would have meant to us now! We had been averaging twelve to fourteen hours a day of walking in the snow. In Blechhamer on Sundays, we had had a shower and even a rest period. As I looked around at what had become of us, I saw a mass of huddled bodies, struggling to lift their feet, their ghost-like faces covered with blankets.

There was talk that we would reach the camp of Gross-Rosen in one day. The guards selected about a hundred men, who couldn't march in step and who appeared sick, and put them on horse-drawn wagons. They were told they would be taken to Gross-Rosen ahead of us. About an hour later, one of those taken on the wagon slipped back and reported that they had been taken to a cemetery and shot. He had escaped.

That night we passed the concentration camp of Peterswalden, which held twelve thousand Jewish women who worked in large textile mills. Some of my inmates' sisters or mothers were in this camp. Who knew what would become of them?

The guards said that we would reach Gross-Rosen that night. It was late, and we were dragging ourselves through the snow. I saw a road sign for Gross-Rosen, but there was no camp in sight. Then we saw blinking lights coming from a tower. Was this it? An end to our sufferings? No matter what kind of camp it was, we reasoned, it had to be better than our present situation.

Chapter 12- K-Z Gross-Rosen

At last, two weeks after leaving Blechhamer we entered the camp. On both sides of the gates stood SS guards, who struck the prisoners at random with their clubs. Although it was the middle of the night, there were so many floodlights that it looked like bright daylight. Why were we being beaten? Who could understand? One SS guard threw out a welcome greeting, "Here you will be finished." Surprisingly, the prisoner next to me, Wroclawski, a tinsmith from Bendzin, answered back, "We are not afraid. Death does not frighten us." This was a daring answer, full of risks, but he was so fed up he probably didn't care any more. Since we were still walking, he was beyond the reach of the SS animal. Wroclawski had worked with me in Cobelwitz in the blacksmith shop. Working there had meant being less tightly guarded and having the chance to develop a relationship with the other, non-Jewish workers. It often meant an extra piece of bread. Even the German supervisor at the shop couldn't stand our hungry, imploring eyes and would break off a piece of bread, throwing it toward us.

As we entered the camp, the local non-Jewish kapos pushed us with their clubs into an area where our feet became mired in the muddy and limey ground. As we struggled to walk in this mud, the brutal kapos screamed, "Faster, you damn gangsters, you bandits, move, move." As they saw us falling, they laughed sadistically. We became so shocked that we thought this must be the end. This was exactly how they wanted us, completely terrorized. I thought, "Those beasts. How can they do this to defenseless people?" The entire population of Blechhamer, minus those who had died on the road, was put into two unfinished brick barracks, two stories high, without windows.

The ground floor had no wooden floor covering the limey mud. The second floor had a cement floor, but it was much colder there, and the wind was much stronger. It was after midnight, and I found a corner to lie down and sleep. Gross-Rosen had been our hope to recover from the past weeks of marching in the worst winter weather. Our reception was a bitter disappointment. We had been dragged here only to end up in these terrible conditions. This place was worse than the barns. I couldn't comprehend it.

At 5 A.M. the kapos started screaming, "Up, you bastards!" Covered with our blankets, we lined up in front of the barracks. Not all of us came out for the roll call. Some had died during the night, freezing to death. They lay there, covered with their blankets. The kapos started the counting, first the live prisoners, then the dead ones, making sure the total number added up to yesterday's count. We stood there for a few hours, our feet stuck in the limey mud. To prevent my feet from freezing, I performed various movements of my toes inside my shoes. I was in agony, standing for a few hours, shivering from the cold and inwardly screaming in pain. Again the dead were being "relieved" of their shoes and blankets by other prisoners. We were now part of a camp, called Camp #2, consisting of about twelve thousand prisoners. Around noon they completed the counting. The roll call leader warned us that next time we could not appear at roll call with our blankets. The blankets must remain in the barracks.

Around 4P.M. we were called to the kitchen, where each of us received a liter of watery soup with some grass or weeds in it. There was no bread. We were told that there would be another soup at 2A.M., in the middle of the night. In the evening bread was brought in, and a three-pound loaf was divided among six prisoners. Not everyone received his or her bread. The kapos, mostly Germans, Ukrainians, and Poles, pocketed the bread of the sick prisoners. While we ate, Ukrainian and Russian prisoners entered our barracks, allegedly to barter, but in reality they grabbed a bowl of soup here and there and ran out. We didn't know how to deal with these thieves until some older Jewish prisoners from Camp #1 told us what to do. As the food was being divided, a few of us positioned ourselves at the door, armed with cut-up boards, sticks, or rocks. As the thieves came in we beat them. They didn't come back that day anymore.

I had been sleeping for a short time when suddenly, around midnight, I heard screams. I received a blow to my head from a wooden club. It was the German senior block elder, grabbing prisoners to bring in the soup. The soup arrived an hour later and was distributed. However we could all see that some soup remained in the kettle. That soup had become the property of the German senior block elder, who wore the green triangle of the professional criminal. The next night, we had the same trouble with the Ukrainians again. I heard a prisoner screaming, "They are stealing my bread!" and another, "They are taking my blanket!" A few of us got up, and we saw a group of Ukrainians stripping the blankets off the sick prisoners, and searching for their bread. The Ukrainians were armed with rocks and metal files. We had a hard time chasing them out. Some of us had bloodied hands and faces, but if we hadn't stood up to them they would have stolen the bread from each one of us. Prisoners from the other barracks told us that the Ukrainian or Russian prisoners had attacked them in the same way.

The three nights we spent at Gross-Rosen were terrible. There was no place to sleep. At 2A.M. the soup was distributed. At 5A.M. we had to get up for the roll call, which meant standing for hours in the bitter cold, our feet deep in the lime. We were never once able to wash our hands or faces. The senior block elder, the German criminal, was constantly beating us, like a wild animal. On the third night, a few of us obtained some wooden boards on which we lay down to sleep. This was an improvement over the limey ground. However it was so bitter cold that night that sleep was impossible. We moaned through the night.

Later that night I heard the senior block elder screaming and saw his club swinging at the heads of those near him. A few officials from the camp office appeared and began registering the Jews. Each of us had to give his or her name and Auschwitz-Blechhamer number. Then we were taken to the camp gate. This was all done with dazzling speed. The senior block elder told us that we were being sent back to Auschwitz. We were confused. I saw to it that the prisoners I knew remained in a tight group, so that we would be in a position to react as a group to whatever happened.

We were divided into groups of one hundred and waited until 5 A.M., when, to our surprise, we received some soup, two pounds of bread per person, a piece of margarine, and a small piece of sausage. This was very unusual. We thought this must be for a long trip. At the food distribution area, there was a Jew, an "old timer" of this camp, who quietly told us that we were being transported to Buchenwald. Later, in the locked railroad cars, our guards told us the same.

We walked out of the camp about 8 P.M. in the direction of the railroad station. As we walked I saw everyone eating, spreading the margarine on the bread, a sight I hadn't seen in a very long time. Some prisoners ate their entire rations right away and then went hungry for the next three days. Others divided the bread as best they could, in order to make it last longer. As we stood outside the gates of Gross-Rosen, we remarked that it was much better to be leaving this camp, for if we had had to stay another week few of us would have remained alive. This place was a real hell. The last night there, several people had rushed at the electric fence, thereby committing suicide. We had been there only three days, yet a few hundred of us from Blechhamer had died.

Chapter 13- Deeper into Germany

When we arrived at the railroad station, cattle cars were waiting for us. The new transport leader, a young Nazi, swung his club around to demonstrate his power. He squeezed eighty-five prisoners into a cattle car. There was standing room only. If we didn't move fast enough he beat our heads and faces. At first we couldn't sit down, but later we found a way to rest our bodies. It was windy and cold. We covered ourselves with our blankets, which were our only protection against the cold. Very few of us had warm underwear. The cars were open on top. After four hours of waiting, the train finally moved. As our bodies leaned against each other, I looked at the passing houses, fields, woods, vast empty spaces, and more houses without end. Germany must be big, I thought. It still has so much territory. I had never been in Germany before. The night air was freezing, and the fatigue from the last three nights of not sleeping overwhelmed me. I fell asleep in a seated position with the blanket covering my head. Conversations had ceased and the only sound was the click-click of the train hitting the rail joints. Those of us who had any bread left hid it under our shirts to protect it from thieves.

I was awakened several times by the cries of those whose bread was stolen. These were heart-rending cries. The victims had tears in their eyes. There were some cases when the rest of us would chip in to help the unfortunate victim. We did this when the inmate was regarded as a decent person, something we could judge after knowing him for a while. There were also some who faked cries of bread being stolen. Such people could expect no help from us. We sensed who the fakers were.

A thin rain drizzled down on us, and our blankets were wet and unpleasant. Yet I felt that it would be worse without them. Thus we sat pressed together, half asleep, half on guard. The train continued its slow ride deeper into Germany, to an unknown new place. Even the guards in the adjoining cars had fallen asleep. It would have been easy to escape with just one jump, but where to? There was no place to run, no friends or allies on the outside, just enemies, heartless beings. Yet they looked like human beings. I saw many civilians, all normal looking people. After several years of being a prisoner, I believed that the world outside was similar to our world inside: prisoners and guards, slaves and masters.

Each time we stopped at a station, I saw men, women, and children walking as in an ordinary life, a life that was but a faint memory to me. I looked out of the car and saw people talking to each other calmly, gently, wives waiting to welcome their husbands, couples embracing. Could this be true? Was this reality? They were only twenty or thirty feet away, yet it seemed as if I was viewing another world, a mirage. Otherwise how could it be that none of them saw us? They looked in our direction yet didn't show the slightest reaction. Didn't they see the injustice done to us? Didn't they have any compassion? Perhaps they regarded us as animals being transported in cattle cars. They walked by with luggage in hand, so close they almost touched the cars, yet they seemed not to notice us. Not one of them stopped even for a moment to look at us. Their world didn't recognize our existence.

The train moved out of the station, and the pain of this of indifference was over. We were again moving through open fields and vast empty stretches of land. What I had witnessed at the station continued to bother me. Would this nightmare ever end? Why were they dragging our half-dead bodies in these trains? Didn't they have more important uses for the trains? I couldn't think of an answer that made any sense. I saw around me a mass of bodies, almost as if welded together, seemingly at peace. It was quiet throughout the train.

Although it was February, dawn came early. We had no idea what time it was or even what day of the week. It mattered not. Protruding from the blankets were strange faces- bearded, eyes recessed, skeletons rather than humans. The prisoners started to move around, rubbing one another with their backs to get their blood circulating again. We tried to clean the blankets of the dirt and mud that remained from Gross-Rosen. Some prisoners didn't move from under their blankets. We uncovered them and saw that they were dead, stiff and frozen. We threw their bodies from the moving train. The guards didn't object. I was later told that in some cases this was prohibited. They had to strictly adhere to the order to deliver the same number of prisoners that had begun the journey, dead or alive. In that case the guards would stack the dead bodies in a corner of the car and cover them with blankets.

We approached the well-known city of Leipzig. Soon the train stopped at the station. I was always among the first to look around and observe a place, although this was officially forbidden. A guard might take aim at you. On the platform I saw men and women, elegantly dressed. They were aware of our presence but avoided looking at us. After their first look, their eyes turned in other directions. Perhaps they thought we were diseased, or worse. Some of us dared to ask the civilians for water. "No, it is forbidden," came the answer. Some didn't even bother to respond. Above our heads, German electricians were repairing the electric wires. They pretended not to see us. Were they really so cold and cruel? Even a stone would be moved by our appearance. Then I saw Red Cross sisters moving around the station, handing out coffee and rolls to the voyagers who were not prisoners. My eyes widened with excitement. Wasn't the Red Cross supposed to help all the needy? While a guard's attention was focused elsewhere, I asked a Red Cross sister, who passed near my car, for some water. She looked at me for a moment, without expression, and kept walking. To the next passing sister, I extended my tin can, so it would be easier to put water or coffee into it. Again there was no reaction. Apparently I had been mistaken about the Red Cross.

Death March To Buchenwald

Then I heard groups of German civilians standing on the platform, pointing to us and saying "Jews, Jews." During the hour or two we waited at the Leipzig rail station, we received not one morsel of food or water, despite our begging. I just couldn't comprehend it. The train finally left the station, ending our hope of getting something to drink. We had no other choice but to lick the snow from the surface of the railcar.

We passed through several cities. At night we sat on the floor, huddled together to retain as much body heat as possible. The bitter, cold wind penetrated the blankets into every part of our bodies. All we could do was to tighten the blankets around us. All of us in the train, including the formerly privileged kapos, and block and room elders, had one thing on our mind. We dreaded the oncoming winter night.

For some it was their last night. In the morning we counted the dead. There were six older prisoners and two young boys, looking as if they were asleep. As we passed the city of Halle, the train slowed down but didn't stop. It seemed to be in the center of Germany. There were no signs of evacuation or of German refugees. We saw workers and soldiers walking peacefully. In Silesia we had seen roads clogged with refugees. As we viewed this scene of serenity and normalcy, we became pessimistic. Perhaps they could continue this war for a very long time. Our situation was critical. Each night brought us closer to death.

Chapter 14- Weimar

The next day a few more prisoners froze to death. This created more space in the railcar, and more blankets were available for those remaining. Around noon we arrived in the city of Weimar. At the Weimar rail station we were told that our destination, the camp of Buchenwald, was ten kilometers away and that a shuttle train would take us there. While we waited for the shuttle, we heard sirens warning of an air raid. In Blechhamer I had been through several air raids. Blechhamer was hit several times, causing serious damage to the factory. During one raid, I thought we were finished. The bomb, which fell not far from me, must have weighed five hundred pounds. I was lying on the ground, desperately holding on to the grass, yet the pressure in the air lifted me several feet high and dropped me down. Many times we had heard the sirens but nothing happened in our area. The planes just passed by, on their way to another destination.

A loudspeaker announced that enemy planes had penetrated the Weimar area. A few minutes later I saw a silvery "bird" flying high up, then two, then four and soon there were too many to count. The sight of these planes in the sky remains very vivid. As an oppressed slave, a Jew, barely staying alive under the ruthless power of the Nazis, I had seen no one able to stop them and their senseless atrocities. This sign of another power in the world, coming down from the skies, appeared to me as a mystical force. It was the first acknowledgement that there was something the Nazis were afraid of and could not control.

Since the beginning of the war, I had seen the Germans as all-powerful and always victorious. Suddenly, here in the midst of Germany, I saw something different. I saw Germans and SS guards running in panic, screaming in fear, like other human beings. To the miserable skeletons in the railcar, this was uplifting. A faint smile made its way from one prisoner to another.

This winter day was bright and clear. White snow covered everything in sight. After a minute the planes came down lower and lower, and I could hear the roaring of their engines. It was like a constant buzzing of bees. As they came closer, they looked like shiny silvery eagles. The antiaircraft sirens on the ground wailed like injured wild beasts, even before anything came out of the planes. We all looked up at the sky. The planes were like an orderly parade. Suddenly we saw little objects the size of snowballs coming out of them. In a minute a series of explosions ripped the air around us. Everything became dark, and clouds of dust and dirt covered the ground. I could count only the first few explosions, then I could no longer count, there were so many. The earth around me was moving up and down. I felt lifted up, with the railcar as well. I couldn't see. Everything around me was black. I heard the roaring of the planes' engines again and repeated explosions. The SS guards and German civilians ran away from the train and hid in the nearest air shelter. Jews were not allowed into the air shelters. Whoever had the strength ran out of the train into the fields, away from the station, which was obviously the target of the bombing.

After a while the explosions subsided. People started to come out, and we heard the cries of the injured, who called for help. Some of the railcars were destroyed or overturned. Others were full of sand and rocks. The rails were bent into different shapes. As the dust started to settle, more people came out.

The planes began to swoop down on us again. The noise of their engines became louder and louder. They came even lower this time. There were more bombs than before. Again the earth trembled, and everything around me became black.

I couldn't run because I didn't have enough strength to climb over the railcar wall. Some of my companions made it. I felt my heart beating so fast I thought it would burst. Then a bomb exploded near our railcar, and a wave of sand, stones, and rocks descended upon us. For a moment I had no idea whether I was alive or dead. I lay there, semi-paralyzed. A heavy rock had hit my thigh, and a smaller one had hit my head. I felt warmth over my entire body and thought that perhaps it was blood flowing over me. I moved my hand to see if I had any strength left and touched my head and legs to see if there was any blood. Only a little blood flowed from my head. My leg, however, was numb and could not move. Next to it was the rock that had hit it. I felt lucky that it hadn't hit my head.

The planes were flying away in the same uniform pattern they had arrived in. Now human cries could be heard everywhere. German civilians were taken to the hospital. As for us, nobody cared who was injured or dead. The female prisoners from the first cars came running to see if their relatives were still alive. Their cars had not been hit so badly as ours. They helped to bind up the open, bloody wounds of those still alive.

Part of the front wall of the railcar I was in was ripped open, and I could see everything in front of me. The area looked different. There were large holes in the ground with water in them, where they had not been before, and hills had appeared out of nowhere. Some of the buildings were gone. There were railcars lying around, damaged. Broken rifles were lying in the mud. Only half of the railroad station house was left. To think that all this had occurred within just a few minutes.

We started to gather the dead bodies. This time the victims were young as well as old. Some cars had more casualties than others. Some bodies were without heads or limbs. Several German guards were also among the dead.

The prisoners had to go back to the railcars. Around me I saw a few heads of cabbage. We ate them quickly.

I felt very disheartened because I couldn't move my leg. I realized what that meant - the end of the road. I would have to say goodbye to the world. I recalled those prisoners whose legs became swollen during the march. They, too, knew their fate was sealed and that nothing could be done about it.

A friend and I exchanged looks, saying nothing. My anxiety, however, lasted only a few minutes. I decided to massage the leg vigorously, and I put some cabbage leaves over the injured area, which had become black. After a while I felt sensations in my leg returning. I tried to see if anything was broken, but I couldn't because of the pain I experienced when I touched it.

In the afternoon we were transferred to another train, which was to take us to Buchenwald. We met some prisoners from Buchenwald who were working in Weimar. As they passed us they informed us that the camp was fairly well organized, and that there was daily distribution of food, which consisted of a hot meal and bread with margarine. As we waited in the railcars my leg began to feel better, and I was able to walk with a limp.

I looked around for Yosef, Nitzah's brother, but there was no trace of him. During the bombing we had become separated. He had stayed close to me during the entire journey. Yosef was several years younger than I, and I knew that his toes were half frozen. I hoped that if he had survived the bombing he might find some help in Buchenwald.

Very late that night the train started moving slowly towards the camp. Both sides of the road were lined with a thick growth of trees, as in a forest. We traveled for over an hour until we arrived at the camp's rail station. It was after midnight and bitterly cold. The train stopped, and orders came to leave the cars. The cars doors were opened, and we had to line up in front of them. I was shocked to see so few prisoners come out. The shouting of the guards didn't help much. The prisoners who remained in the cars were either unable to move or were dead. Slowly the train was emptied.

We had left Blechhamer a month ago, with four thousand five hundred men and two hundred women. When we arrived at Buchenwald we were approximately four to five hundred. It was February 1945, and from Blechhamer to Buchenwald there was a long trail of our dead. Our murdered brothers had been caught in this monstrous, insane system of brutality and inhumanity. The bloodstained snow on the roads leading from the concentration camps of Eastern Europe into Germany testified to the tens of thousands of human beings murdered by other human beings, imbued with a degenerate philosophy of nationalism and racial superiority. A special breed of humanity.

Arriving in Buchenwald was the last part of our evacuation. Many of us would die there. For others the same agony was to continue on the roads of Germany for another few months.

Chapter 15- K-Z Buchenwald, Human Solidarity in Hell

When we arrived in Buchenwald, I expected a horde of kapos to swoop down on us screaming and swinging with their clubs – the usual reception. Instead prisoners approached us and helped us to get off the train. Instead of hearing the usual, "Fast, fast, you dogs, you shit," we were spoken to like human beings. It was another world I had once known but whose existence I had forgotten. These prisoners even assured us that the camp had a hospital and medical facilities for the sick. This was so unbelievable that I thought it was another trick. The prisoners wore better-quality striped uniforms and looked healthier than we did. I thought they must be kapos or other camp officials very close to the SS. They wore reds triangles and spoke unaccented German. They were political prisoners, opponents or resisters of Nazism. When some inmates who could barely walk were picked out to go to the camp infirmary, I thought they were being selected for death. I could hardly believe it when I saw them later, alive.

The only German prisoners I had ever met in the camps wore a green triangle, the professional criminals. In camps whose prisoners were mostly Jewish, the SS gave the criminals high positions of authority and privilege. They were better dressed and better fed than the rest of us. They were used by the Nazis to torture and terrorize other prisoners. They were great sadists and often beat prisoners to death. However, because they were Aryans they belonged to the "superior" race. When speaking to us they used the same insults as the SS--"you Jewish warmongers, you Jewish swine."

When we arrived, we were placed into the "small camp." This consisted of a group of twelve barracks, separated from the main camp and surrounded by barbed wire. These barracks had no windows. A triple layer of wooden platforms, which served as beds, lined the walls from one end to the other. There was very little or no straw on these platforms. Prisoners were dying on them. Into these barracks the Nazis pushed about fifteen hundred prisoners. Sanitary conditions were awful. Water was available only occasionally from the half-inch pipes outside the barracks. One had to stand in a long line to get a little water to drink or to wash oneself with.

We were given showers, had our heads shaved, and received clean uniforms. Our old uniforms had deteriorated into rags. Some of the very sick prisoners, who perhaps could have been helped, refused to go to the infirmary, fearing that it was really a liquidation area.

On the second day, the old-timers told us that the food was divided equally and that stealing another prisoner's bread would be severely punished by the prisoner leadership. Later old-timers from the main camp appeared and asked us to point out the brutal kapos and guards from Blechhamer, or from the march, who had mistreated prisoners. They also wanted to know which officials stole food from prisoners. Some of the kapos were taken away, and from what we heard, the prisoner underground was investigating them. Some of the most brutal ones never returned to the barracks. We were told they had paid for their crimes.

I soon got the impression that a secret prisoner organization was a moving force within this camp and that this organization had representatives of various nationalities, even Jews. After Gross-Rosen this was a surprise to me. The deputy senior block elder of block 66, the children's block, was Gustav Schiller. He was a Polish Jew and a Communist. We liked and respected him. Many of the complaints about brutal behavior that had occurred in the other camps went to him. His block contained over one thousand prisoners, mostly Jewish youngsters from Poland, Hungary, Romania, and other countries. He was in charge of the distribution of food, and he kept it as equal as possible. This was a far cry from what we had known in other camps. But this was not the case in all the barracks. In those chaotic conditions many injustices were committed, probably because the underground could not assert its power completely.

The warm meals and daily bread rations helped me to recover a little strength. I even volunteered with another dozen prisoners from my block to bring the soup kettles from the kitchen. I did this for two reasons. First, the porters received an additional portion of soup, and secondly, I was curious to see what the main camp was like. The main camp, which housed the permanent prisoners of Buchenwald, seemed to me to be cleaner and more orderly than the small camp. Some of the barracks in the main camp were cement block structures.

Chapter 16- Block 49, Walter from Saarbrucken

On one of these trips to carry the soup kettles, I became acquainted with the senior block elder of the German political prisoners. His name was Walter Sonntag, and he seemed to be a very serious person, very different from the sadistic Walter at Blechhamer. He told me that his block was #49, which was at the end of the permanent camp and close to the small camp. The next time we met, he told me that he came from Saarbrucken, an industrial city near the French-German border.

We started talking politics, and it came out in the discussion that I had been an active Socialist like my father. My father was a well-known Socialist-Zionist leader in the city of Alexandrov, near Lodz. Lodz was the largest industrial city in Poland. My father had also been one of the early organizers of the resistance to the pogroms of 1936-37, which had been inspired and sanctioned by the semi-fascist Polish government. He had a reputation as a daring, courageous man.

I remember he came home once with a bloodied face and torn clothing. He told us what had happened. He had been riding home in the train from Lodz, in a car with two drunken Poles who were pulling the beards and earlocks of Hasidic Jewish men. This was not an unusual event in those days. Jew-hating Poles often amused themselves in this way. Although the Hasidim outnumbered the Poles in the railcar, as well as in Alexandrov, they usually did not fight back but tried to evade the thugs by walking away. Such had been their mentality for centuries. However this railcar was closed, and there was nowhere to run. My father, who because of his modern attire was not molested, could not stand to witness the abuse and told the Poles to stop. They gave him a look of contempt and continued to amuse themselves, pulling the beards of the black-garbed Hasidim. My father struck one of the Poles with his hand. They were astounded that a Jew had dared to hit them, and they turned on him. My father was a muscular, well-developed man and defended himself ably. The two surprised Poles pulled the emergency brake, and when the train stopped they ran out screaming, "Jews are attacking Christians!" They called out to Poles in the other railcars to help them. Many Poles joined them, and soon my father was being severely beaten. Not a single Hasid came to his aid. They all disappeared.

During 1937-38 the racist, semi-fascist Polish government, encouraged by Nazi actions in Germany, had organized pogroms against the Jews in several cities. This followed the measures taken by the Polish government to destroy the Jewish community economically. Jews began to organize self-defense units in many cities. The need for defense was particularly apparent after the pogrom in the city of Pczytyk, where thousands of peasants from the surrounding areas came to rob, plunder, and murder the Jewish community. Official government circles openly encouraged this pogrom.

The Jewish community leaders, who were the representatives of the Zionist and non-Zionist political parties, elected my father to head the defense organization of Alexandrov, where his family had lived for hundreds of years. This bleak development was soon overshadowed by the Nazi invasion.

After a while, Walter asked me if I would like to transfer from my block in the small camp to his block in the permanent camp. Naturally I agreed, since the living conditions in the permanent camp were much better. In the small camps, transports were being formed to leave for other, satellite camps of Buchenwald. At the same time new transports were arriving from the east, far beyond the capacity of the small camp. People were dying daily. The danger of typhoid was real despite the best efforts of the camp underground. Walter transferred me to his barracks, block #49. Another reason I was glad to be transferred was that I hoped that, out of this block, I would be able to work in Weimar, and get a chance to look around. Prisoners from the small camp were not being sent to work outside Buchenwald, since they were considered "temporary." I very much wanted to see the outside world, so I volunteered to go to Weimar with the work details at 5 A.M. each morning. I thought that being part of the work details might protect me from being sent on a transport out of Buchenwald, which I wanted very much to avoid.

Block #49, my new living quarters, was a large two-story cement building. To transfer someone there from the small camp wasn't easy, and Walter must have pulled some strings in the camp office, where the underground had strong influence. He must have given them a reason for the transfer. Since no monetary considerations existed, the only reason could have been my identification as a Socialist and the value these people placed on it. Perhaps also potential need of such people in the future.

In block #49 I learned how this highly secret prisoner organization operated, under the noses of the SS, to influence the inner life of the camp. It maintained a high moral standard of relations between prisoners of various nationalities. To me this was fantastic. I admired it and would have joined immediately, if asked, even with the personal risk it involved. These prisoners were the most conscious and principled enemies of Nazism. They understood what they struggled for and why they must never give up.

Chapter 17 - Hunger

In Weimar the work detail cleaned up the rubbish of the bombed-out houses and dug under the ruins to find bodies. I felt fortunate because being outside the camp daily was a great lift for me. I could see the civilian population, the stores, their life and the streets. I hadn't seen these things in a long time. Although we were strictly forbidden to look and were constantly under the watchful eye of the guard, we managed to see.

We were woken up at 5A.M. and received eight ounces of bread. This had to last till 7P.M. when we returned to the camp and got some soup. How to live on this food allotment, how to divide it up – this was the question that plagued our conversations daily. We each had different theories, looking for solutions that didn't exist. We were all so hungry, and this portion of bread was not enough to sustain life. The problem was how to make it last till evening. Those prisoners who were able to divide the bread into two or three portions showed the strongest will power. They ate the first piece in the morning, put the rest back into their pocket, removed the carefully wrapped bread a few hours later for lunch, and again at 4P.M. Such strong willed people were very rare among us. The rest of us vowed each morning to follow this regimen, but couldn't. Hunger won out over our resolve.

I too vowed that I would follow the regimen. It was the only rational way to survive, I told myself. At 5A.M. when I received the bread, I broke off a piece and spread the margarine over it. I promised myself not to touch the rest until lunchtime. We stood at the large central square where we were counted, and waited to depart. We were waiting over an hour. It was cold and the bread in my pocket teased me. That square of margarine had been so good, that it had inflamed my intestines. My stomach was again empty and was crying for more. Those few bites I had taken earlier had only served to stimulate my hunger. A struggle took place within me. Finally, not being to stand it any longer, I reached into my pocket, took out the bread and broke off half with a vengeance. I cleaned my mouth with my tongue sucking up every little piece so that nothing remained. Immediately after this I was angry with myself. Why had I done it? That piece was meant to be eaten at lunch. I had lost this round to my biggest enemy, Hunger.

We still stood in the square, waiting. Another 15 minutes passed. Every minute I touched my pocket to check if the bread hadn't been stolen. The constant touching of the bread and the recurring hunger wouldn't leave me alone. Again I struggled within myself, to eat or not? I stopped touching it and felt proud of myself. Suddenly I saw a Russian prisoner passionately biting into his entire portion. He really enjoyed it and finished it in a minute. My resolve of a moment ago vanished. I couldn't stand it. I ripped apart the last piece with my teeth and held the last piece in my mouth as long as possible. Finally there was no more. At 6A.M. we hadn't yet started out for work and my bread for the entire day was already gone.

At 9A.M. our detail worked at removing bricks and cement slabs from the buildings and piling them into trucks. Some of the prisoners started to eat. I stood and stared. Then I tore my eyes away and resumed my work. Again I vowed not to do tomorrow what I had done today. I argued with myself, trying to convince my "decision maker". Wouldn't it have been better if I too had something to eat now, even only a bite, instead of going hungry all day long? I could only hope to find a piece of bread or potato among the ruins as I sometimes had in the past.

At lunchtime, with my last strength, I raised the sledgehammer. It was so hard. I was so weak and tired. My anger at myself flared up again. Why had I eaten the entire portion this morning? Why hadn't I resisted?

Death March To Buchenwald

I still had to work another six hours. It was already dark and I was barely able to lift the shovel. We all looked at the nearby church clock, moving so slowly. If only it would move a little faster. I was so hungry. Tomorrow, I promised myself, I will not eat the entire portion in the morning. I will resist temptation and my enemy, Hunger.

The next morning the same struggle repeated itself and again it is Hunger who won, not I. At lunchtime I again vowed not to give in. Day after day the struggle of my stomach against my will power continued – over the piece of bread in my pocket.

Chapter 18- The Underground- Political Prisoners

The weak don't fight
The strong fight perhaps an hour
The exceptionally strong fight for many years,
But those whose strength is truly heroic fight all their lives;
To them we are indebted, for they are indispensable
-Bertold Brecht

Buchenwald had not always been like this. For years, vicious German criminal prisoners had ruled its life. It had at first been a camp for Germans only. The criminal prisoners brutalized the political prisoners and sent many of them to their death. Their behavior pleased the SS officials. The criminals viewed the political prisoners as fools and called them traitors to the Fatherland, Bolsheviks, etc. They beat Jews to death at the slightest provocation. It was an amazing story of human courage: these German antifascists, Socialists, and Communists wrested the power from the criminal element to administer the inner life of the camp.

The struggle to obtain the top job of senior camp elder was a desperate struggle for life and death that often required deadly methods to overcome the ruthlessness of the criminals. What helped the political prisoners was that the criminals were unreliable and easily corrupted.

Another thing about the political prisoners impressed me. This was the first time since the Nazis came to power that I had seen a group of Germans treating Jews as human beings. In the ghetto and the various camps I had been in, I thought there were no decent Germans left, with the exception of Sergeant Kopicky from Bobrek and the peasant girl, Lena, at Cobelwitz. This was especially true during the evacuation from Blechhamer. During that march, whenever I was lucky enough to receive food from peasants, I never let them know that I was Jewish. I spoke fluent German and pretended to be a Catholic Pole or Dutchman. I usually covered the Jewish star on my chest with a long scarf. Twice farmers had chased me out when they noticed the Jewish star. For a Jew they could not find the compassion to offer a piece of bread.

In block #49 a different atmosphere prevailed. Antisocial, egotistic behavior was not tolerated. Even the criminal prisoners in that block were kept in check. They knew if they ratted to the SS they might end up dead.

The next block, #50, was not a typical block because it did not house prisoners. When I asked Walter what was in there, he sternly cautioned me, saying, "If you ever get there, you are finished, so stay away." I had no idea that block #50 was used for medical experiments. Prisoners were injected with typhoid in hopes of producing a serum for the German army. Hundreds of prisoners, men and women, died in the course of these experiments.

I became aware of this only after liberation, when I read Dr. Eugene Kogon's book on Nazi concentration camps, based mainly on his experience at Buchenwald. Experiments on prisoners with malaria injections were also conducted in block #50. Dr. Kogon was an Austrian and an anti-Nazi liberal. He was somehow able to influence the chief Nazi doctor, Dr. Ding-Schuler, and became his confidant. Since Nazi officials dreaded entering this block, important prisoners whose life was in imminent danger could find a hiding place there.

Dr. Ding-Schuler was also in charge of block #46, which was the original typhoid experimentation block. This block was strictly isolated and surrounded with barbed wire. According to Dr. Kogon, about one thousand prisoners were deliberately infected with typhoid and malaria. Most of them died. Most victims of these experiments were homosexuals, criminals, and Polish clergymen.

When I learned how close I had been to this monstrous block I shuddered. The tragic thing was that it was the prisoners themselves, well-known medical authorities from various European countries, who were forced to conduct the experiments. Their medical expertise kept the Nazis from killing them.

Reich Physician, Dr. Grawitz, headed the entire program of medical experiments on prisoners in the various camps. He was also the personal physician to Himmler, as well as his friend. After the war he was sentenced to death during the Nazi medical trial in 1947, together with Professor Karl Brandt, Hitler's personal physician. Dr. Ding-Schuler was apprehended in September 1945 and committed suicide in prison. Unfortunately most Nazi doctors who murdered thousands of prisoners escaped justice and went unpunished.

In Weimar as we removed the debris from bombed-out buildings, carted it away, and searched for dead bodies, the kapo of the work detail, a political prisoner, never beat anyone. He apportioned the work according to each prisoner's ability. We had the greatest respect for and confidence in him. We always brought to his attention anything unusual we found digging in the ruins. As soon as he was able to obtain food, he divided it as fairly as possible among us. Only after liberation did I discover that this work detail was part of the underground.

Walter, the senior block elder, was in his late forties or early fifties. We became friendlier after I was transferred to his block. He told me the story of how the politicals had succeeded in gaining power over the criminals and how some of his best friends had lost their lives in the struggle. At one point when the administration of the inner camp had shifted to the politicals, the entire political camp leadership was summoned to the gate and executed. The SS had been able to infiltrate the politicals with a spy. Among the executed were editors of newspapers, members of the pre-Hitler German parliament, and leaders of the Socialist and Communist parties.

It took time until a new leadership evolved and resumed the struggle against the criminals in the camp administration. They succeeded and in

1944 the camp administration was again in the hands of the red triangles. Whenever Walter related these events to me he always looked around to make sure his deputy block elder was not around. The deputy wore a green triangle. He was a young man in his early twenties with a distinct Viennese accent. Even at this time in 1945, some criminal prisoners still held high positions, but in block #49 Walter was the boss.

Walter had a small office. It consisted of a table and a few chairs and was located near the main entrance door. This enabled him to keep an eye on whoever entered or left the block. At this table he also did his clerical work. One day as I approached Walter's office, I overheard a conversation about me between Walter and his criminal deputy. The deputy asked in an angry voice why I had been transferred from the small block into this block. He must have noticed that Walter often spoke to me, and this made him angry. When Walter explained that he liked me because I was the type of person who fit into this block, alluding to the political nature of our relationship, the deputy burst out, "And you believe him? He is lying. They (Jews) are all lying." The deputy was clearly a Jew-hater, as were most of the green triangles. Walter steered the conversation into a different direction. I realized then how careful I had to be, to watch out for this criminal. Although he was not the boss of the block, nevertheless he could do me great harm.

I stayed in this block almost until the end of the war, during the most critical days of my struggle for survival, except for the last five or six days, when no Jew could remain in the block. As for Walter, he never disappointed me. He remained true to his humanity, to his antifascist principles. He could easily have put me on a transport list to another camp and have avoided bad blood with the deputy. Later, in the crucial last days before the Nazi collapse, Jews were ordered to leave the camp. Senior block elders were to execute the order to remove any Jews from their blocks, but Walter did not betray me.

If it were up to the green triangles, not a single Jew would have survived. They hated us no less than the Nazis and enthusiastically did their dirty work. They had nothing against Nazism and its ideas and often expressed admiration for Hitler.

From time to time I went to visit the small camp. Many of those who had survived the death march from Blechhamer to Buchenwald were sent to other camps. Most of the children and teenagers were sent to block #66 and some to blocks in the large camp. Those who were weak and couldn't move were transferred to Block #61, the block of the incurables. There, I was told, they were given lethal injections by an SS guard. The senior block elders made the selections. They did it rather than let the SS do it. Otherwise many more prisoners would have been selected as incurable.

Chapter 19- The Last Desperate Agony and Liberation

At the beginning of 1945, the fighting was closer to the province of Thuringia, where Buchenwald and many of its satellite camps were located. In April, the large and the small camp, at Buchenwald held over seventy thousand prisoners. The blocks became overcrowded. Each morning, hundred of bodies were carried out of the barracks and stacked in a pile to be taken to the crematory. New transports were no longer allowed in. They were taken to southern Germany.

At the same time we heard the artillery bombardments coming closer, from the west of Buchenwald. The Allies could not be too far off. On our minds was one thought, "Why don't they march faster?" Walter was constantly going to the prison camp administration office. All the senior block elders went there to obtain instructions from the SS and from their own inmate leaders. Actually I knew by then that the core of the underground was located there. Coming back from the office, he would cheer us up with, "It won't take long. The end is in sight." His words made a deep impression on me. I knew he was an honest man and wouldn't just raise empty hopes. It seemed he truly believed what he said. I had long forgotten that such a possibility existed. I was so immersed in the daily struggle that I couldn't think beyond how to survive each day. Walter's words of hope encouraged me to stick it out in Buchenwald.

Inhumanity

As the Allies approached and German defeats multiplied, the minds of the SS camp guards had to be affected. They must have quietly considered the possibility of losing the war. In the early mornings as we were herded from the roll call area to work in the ruins of Weimar, we were surrounded on all sides by guards. I tried to detect some changes in their attitudes through their behavior. I saw no change. They barked their insults and orders automatically. However discipline slackened a little. At the beginning of April the work details stopped going to Weimar. We heard rumors that the western Allies were close by and that the commandant had declared that he would surrender the camp to them. We heard other rumors that the German air force would bomb the camp to the ground with all the prisoners in it.

Suddenly, on April 5, we heard from the loudspeaker, "All Jews to report to the roll call area." Thus the evacuation from Buchenwald began. Senior block elders, as usual, were responsible for the execution of orders. The underground, sensing that this might be the beginning of the total evacuation of the camp, urged the Jews not to cooperate, and many senior block elders told Jews not to report. When only a small number of Jews reported--a few hundred instead of six or seven thousand, the SS officials were shocked and angry. This was probably the first time such an insubordination had occurred in the camp. The SS ordered the Jews to return to the barracks. We had obtained a day's delay in our struggle for survival. Naturally we knew that the camp officials would use brutal methods to impose their will upon the prisoners.

Personally, I knew well what another evacuation would mean. I decided to hide rather than appear at the roll call. I felt that I had little chance to survive another march into southern Germany. I removed the Jewish star from my jacket. From a position where I could view the roll call area, I saw the few hundred Jews who had obeyed the order being dismissed and sent back to their barracks. I didn't remain in the block during the day but slipped back in at night to sleep. I found some empty beds of prisoners hiding elsewhere. My German neighbor was unperturbed since the order to evacuate pertained only to Jews. The German prisoner on the other side was an elderly man who periodically received packages from home. We used to trade things I found in the bombed-out homes in Weimar for a piece of bread or cheese. Ninety percent of my block was non-Jewish. Each morning I left the block because I feared the SS guard would appear, and I would be trapped. I didn't even wait for the food distribution.

During the next few days the SS was able to ferret out about two thousand Jews. They simply surrounded the block, told the prisoners to line up in front, and picked out the Jews. They did this with the help of the green triangles and, sometimes, the senior block elders. On April 8 there were still a few thousand Jews left hiding in the camp.

Suddenly the evacuation of all prisoners was announced. The prisoners of various nationalities were being driven to the gate, which faced the road toward southern Germany. The prisoner underground could not openly resist the evacuation. It would have caused a mass slaughter. During the next few days, the SS evacuated eight to ten thousand prisoners daily. Yet the SS knew that Jews still remained in the camp and were determined to apprehend them.

With my yellow star removed and a red triangle in its place, I often slipped back into block #49 in order to get something to eat. This block had a majority of Germans, and they were scheduled to leave the camp last. Around April 9 I came out of my hiding place and entered the block. Suddenly two SS guards, with pistols drawn, came in and ordered all prisoners to line up in front. The prisoners lined up in rows of four deep, and the SS ordered, "Jews step out." No one moved. They threatened to shoot any Jew who didn't step out voluntarily. Even if I wanted to, I couldn't have stepped forward because I now wore a red triangle with the letter "D" on it, (signaling that I was German.) For this fraud alone, I would have been shot immediately. I feared that another prisoner who knew me would point me out. This had happened in other blocks. The guards then ordered Walter, the senior block elder, to walk with them down the line, look into the prisoners' faces, and identify any Jews. It was the most critical moment in my life, which I will never forget. I regretted having left my hiding place. Standing at attention in the second row, I stared forward with a frozen

Inhumanity

expression. Would Walter point me out? I was sweating as Walter slowly walked by with the SS guards and looked into the faces of the prisoners. His eyes met mine for a split second as he proceeded to the end of the line. "No Jews here," he reported to the Nazis. After the search was over and the SS had left, Walter told me to disappear because too many prisoners in the block knew that I was Jewish. He had in mind the deputy who, fortunately, had been absent during the search.

Relieved, I went back to my hiding place, which was a tool cabinet. Since the beginning of the evacuation all work had stopped, and the large machine halls were empty. They were surrounded by barbed wire and guarded by the camp police. I had found a weak spot in the wire, enlarged it, and slipped into a machine hall. I picked out a large lathe standing in a corner. All large machines had tool cabinets next to them. I transferred the tools inside elsewhere and pressed myself into the cabinet, closing the door from the inside. I could hear the slightest sound of anyone entering the hall.

Once or twice daily an SS guard would have a look around to check the inventory and look for any prisoners trying to hide. I stayed in that cramped position for over two days and three nights. Only at night did I venture out to stretch my body and seek information of what had happened during the day. I was told that the evacuation of the camp was in full swing. Transports of prisoners, except for the German ones, were leaving the camp. Around 5 A.M. on April 11, a camp policeman entered the hall and must have a heard a noise coming from the tool cabinet where I hid. Perhaps I had moved while asleep, because I hadn't heard him coming into the hall. He opened the cabinet, saw me, and warned me to leave or the SS would kill me. He told me that the entire camp was being evacuated.

I was half frozen, hadn't eaten anything for two days, and could hardly move. I roamed the camp, watching for SS guards. Many barracks were now standing empty. The fresh morning air revived me a little. I noticed other shadows moving around between the blocks. At about 9 A.M. I saw a group of German political prisoners standing near a block

Death March To Buchenwald

and quietly discussing the situation. They were looking toward the camp gate and keenly watching any action coming from there. From their conversation I understood that there were still thousands of inmates in the camp, although daily ten to twelve thousand prisoners were being evacuated on foot. These middle-aged Germans were analyzing the situation, and my impression was that they were part of the underground. I kept hanging around to hear more. They ignored my presence and didn't chase me away.

Around 10A.M. the sirens started to wail. We all looked for cover, and I ran into the nearest block. About two hours later, the camp radio ordered all the SS to report to the camp office. This was the beginning of their withdrawal. The main SS officials had already left the camp. The noise of artillery became louder and sounded very close. An alarm sounded and guards left the watchtowers. The main gate was silent. It seemed that they had all left in a hurry. I was later told that some of the SS had looted the warehouse of jewelry and other valuables before leaving. By this time the underground took out their hidden weapons and quietly mounted the watchtowers. A white flag was hung atop the main gate where the Nazi flag had hung before. While this was going on most prisoners were confined to their barracks and were worrying about the evacuation. They were not aware that the Nazis had fled.

At around 2P.M. I heard loud noises coming from the roll call area. I saw prisoners going towards it, shouting joyously, "an American tank!" As I approached I saw a tank with an American soldier on top. Words were exchanged with the soldier, and happiness appeared on the faces of the prisoners there. Yet no one really knew what to say. The tank was part of an advance patrol, and after a while it left.

I was so weak that I could hardly rejoice in the liberation. There was no energy in me for any outward display of emotion. Others, non-Jews, rejoiced a little. For the last week I had been a hunted animal, fighting desperately for life against terrible odds. The SS had been committed to removing every Jew from the camp. Shunned by my fellow prisoners, I wandered at night like a lone dog, retreating into the safety of the tool cabinet for a night's "rest" in a cramped position. Freezing cold surrounded me. Each step I took was full of tension. Each day of the last week was unbearably long. In the end I even lost the cabinet retreat and was forced to roam around in the open. I had to delay, to avoid being part of another march, which I doubted I could survive.

The tension in me subsided little by little. Though still numbed, I felt that things were different now. It seemed true. The Nazi era had come to an end. Yet part of me remained unsure.

Standing in the roll call area after the American tank left, I saw armed inmates bringing in a few SS guards. These were the guards who had manned the watchtowers and been unable to get far enough away. They had been left to guard the camp while the Nazi officials cleared out with the marching prisoners. These Nazis were probably tormenting and killing those prisoners, marching into southern Germany.

I could hardly stand on my feet. For several days I had barely eaten, drinking only some water from the faucet in the machine hall. The cramped position in the cabinet hadn't allowed me to really sleep. Somehow I got a piece of bread, and before I collapsed I went back to block #49, where I fell asleep.

I woke late the next morning. I heard people speaking of soup being given out in the kitchen. I rushed there and received a bowl of hot, thick, fatty soup with meat and other solid food in it--the first good meal I had eaten for a very long time. It was delicious. I finished the bowl and immediately had to rush to the toilet. My stomach had not digested fat for so long, that it reacted violently. I had to return repeatedly to the toilet. I realized that I had contracted dysentery, and I well knew its danger. It could kill me. The next few days were torture. Right after I ate my daily bread ration I had to rush to the toilet. I became steadily weaker and on the fifth or sixth day I lay semiconscious, unable to move. With the help of a block mate, I dragged myself to the camp infirmary. It was packed. There was only one visiting American doctor, who examined me and stated that I was seriously ill and must remain. I collapsed onto the floor and stretched out. The doctor looked down sadly at me and raised his hands, saying, "What can I do? I have no medicines."

Death March To Buchenwald

Many prisoners died of dysentery after liberation. It was widespread within the camp. I appeared to the doctor as a lost cause. After a while I lapsed into unconsciousness. For the next ten days I swung between life and death. Afterwards, reading the labels on the bottles, I saw that I had been given injections of glucose. It had been procured somehow from the German supplies. Slowly I emerged from my stupor. After a couple of weeks I was able to leave the infirmary and return to the block, where I gradually regained strength.

Chapter 20- After Liberation

Each day more and more of my fellow inmates who had survived this hellish place were leaving. They had homes to go to, in their respective countries, where families and friends awaited them. A nation was there to greet them with open arms. I was genuinely happy for them.

For the Jewish survivors, from Poland and other Eastern European countries, it was different. We knew that there were no homes with people in them expecting us. What had not been destroyed had probably been taken over by the local gentiles. There was no nation to welcome us with open arms, just the opposite. Yet, I couldn't decide not to return. Perhaps someone had miraculously survived. However, I didn't have the strength to walk back to Poland and there were no trains running in that direction. My memories of Poland were not pleasant. I remembered as a boy seeing the crowds of Catholic Poles teeming out of the churches Sunday mornings. They came out riled up and agitated, wanting to beat up Jews. They were looking to spill some blood. No Jew had better be on that street at that time. I lived on the street where the church was and often witnessed young Poles attacking Jewish peddlers who had their wares displayed in the marketplace nearby. Their merchandise was destroyed and often plundered.

I had many other bitter experiences with Polish anti-Semitism. One of the most traumatic incidents was one I witnessed in 1938, one year before the war. It happened in Lodz, the second largest city in Poland, on May 3, a Polish national holiday. The extreme right political party was holding a rally in Helenovick Park. As they paraded past my house, I saw they numbered ten to fifteen thousand. My parents and neighbors warned me not to go out into the street. The gate to our apartment building was bolted. But I was curious and looked through a small hole in the gate into the street. I saw a mob marching with clubs in their hands, shouting, "Death to the Jews!" I was shocked and couldn't understand where all these people had come from and why they wanted to kill me. What had we done to them? This was the fascist, racist party called the National Democrats. They often attacked the Polish Socialists.

The sight of these Jew-hating marchers filing past my house for over two hours left an indelible memory. I had been unaware of their existence and could not comprehend it. I was reluctant to go back to this country, whose population had been spoon-fed anti-Semitism for centuries by the Catholic Church. The semi-fascist government used this inbred anti-Semitism. Although Poland had been occupied by the Nazis and had suffered their brutality, there were many Poles who had hunted Jews to deliver them to the Nazis. This too, I couldn't forget.

Each day I said goodbye to the transports of Danish, Dutch, Czech, French, Italian, and other inmates who went home to what I imagined was a warm reception. I wished them well in their work of rebuilding their countries, free of fascism. The speeches on the camp radio urged them to go back and help rebuild their countries. I felt that this appeal did not apply to me, to the Jews.

I became active in the Committee of Liberated Jews in Buchenwald. We had problems with the camp leadership. They could not understand the Jewish problem. They refused to recognize us as a nationality, as legitimate representatives of these inmates, although most Jews identified with us, especially those from Eastern Europe. To them we were Poles, Hungarians, Latvians, etc. They forgot that we didn't suffer as members of these nationalities but were killed because we were Jews. Ours was a common destiny, but they didn't draw the obvious conclusions. A famous saying went, "Not all the victims were Jewish, but all the Jewish prisoners were destined to die." This state of being an eternal minority at the whims of others had to end.

On April 11, 1945, the day of liberation, Buchenwald had about twenty-one thousand prisoners of various nationalities. The figures given at the time by the camp leadership were:

France   5,000
Poland   3,500
Germany   2,200
Russia   2,000
Ukraine   2,000
Czech   2,000
Yugoslavia 600
Holland   400
Austria, Italy, Spain, Norway   200
Other   3,000

There was no recognition of Jews as a nationality or a people. I had to adjust these figures to derive the number of Jews in the camp after liberation. I estimated that there were close to three thousand Jews, nine to eleven hundred of whom were children below the age of eighteen. Some of them were as young as ten years of age.

The Russians were not all prisoners of war. Some were civilians, former laborers. The Russian soldiers were the most mistreated group, after the Jews. Thousands of them were killed in cold blood or left to starve in the camps or on the roads. The German underground, mainly the German Communists, tried to help them with food. If the underground members were caught, they were shot on the spot. The Nazis hated the Russian soldiers intensely and regarded them as subhuman. This was the image they fostered on the German people. I had seen this in the German newspapers I read. One illustrated magazine had on its front cover an image of a Russian soldier as a wild Mongol-type beast, ready to rape and murder. The caption underneath read, "the wild Asiatic Bolsheviks, on a world conquest." I imagined the real reason for the Nazis' hatred was that they could not defeat the Russians. I had overheard the Nazis complaining that there were too many of them and that this was the reason they had not succeeded on the eastern front. In Blechhamer, German disabled soldiers, who had returned from the Russian front, had worked as overseers. They bragged, "We mowed them down by the thousands, and still they kept coming. Russians have too much of a human supply," was their bitter complaint. The Russian war prisoners were kept isolated from all other prisoners, and their executions were kept secret, as were their deaths by starvation. Perhaps hundreds of thousands of them died in this manner.

Ukrainian civilians were a different matter. Some of them, even those who had formerly served in the Russian army, eagerly served the Germans and acted as guards and executioners in the camps. They openly displayed their anti-Semitic tendencies, imitating the Nazis.

Chapter 21 – From Buchenwald into Southern Germany, My Unfortunate Brothers

For those of us who had avoided being evacuated and had remained in Buchenwald, the war ended on April 11, 1945. But for the tens of thousands of prisoners who had been evacuated from Buchenwald and the thousands of other prisoners on the roads heading south toward Dachau and the Tyrolean mountains, the agony continued. Each day meant death for those who could no longer march or succumbed to starvation and cold.

Among them were a number of my friends, who were in the small camp the last few months and were evacuated first, when evacuation affected "Jews only." Their terrible struggle could be felt only by someone who had experienced this hell. Most of them were physically worn down by the previous marches and the time spent in the camps and were already half dead by the time they marched out of Buchenwald. I knew that beyond the gate lay constant confrontation with death. This was why I had been so determined to remain in Buchenwald.

By then the Nazis must have seen clearly that their empire was lost, yet they continued. Perhaps they hoped that the "miracle weapon" promised on their radio broadcasts would turn the war around. Rumors circulated that the Nazis planned to exchange the prisoners in return for their own safety or that they intended to make the Tyrol their last stand and the graveyard of their prisoners.

Death March To Buchenwald

During the last few weeks before liberation, when the camp could no longer hold the arriving transports, they were directed to bypass the camp and head toward Dachau. Dachau soon became overcrowded, and then those transports were added to the others on the roads to the Tyrol.

My friend, Israel Segal, who left Buchenwald on April 6, 1945 in a transport of one thousand six hundred and fifty Jewish prisoners, reported:

Many Jews did not obey the order that came over the loudspeaker to report to the roll call area. The SS had to comb through the camp, especially the small camp to look for the Jews. Those who were apprehended were placed in the large hall of the Gustloff machine plant. We were guarded by the camp police, who wore green triangles, although some wore white armbands. They were the reserve camp police. Apparently the Nazis didn't trust the political prisoners to do this work.

When the Nazis came into our block to search for Jews, they were often helped by our Polish and Ukrainian "comrades," who pushed us into the front row, so that the SS could identify us. We remained for two days in the machine halls without food or water. The weak dropped like flies, and the first day we had seven dead. One corner of the hall became the toilet. Nearby the dead were piled up. The next day an SS doctor announced that we shouldn't worry as we were soon to be transported to Theresienstadt. During the days more Jewish prisoners came into the hall. Some were from the barracks where the SS had apprehended them. Others were from new transports arriving in Buchenwald. That night more died.

At 4A.M. on Friday they woke us up with their clubs, chasing us out in the direction of the gate where they counted us into units of one hundred. The counted us over and over again.

The SS officials chose the healthier prisoners to pull the vehicles with their personal belongings. Another vehicle was loaded with shovels and picks and placed at the end of the transport. This was for those who would not be able to keep up. The guards held vicious dogs, ready to rip us apart. Some of these guards were Ukrainians.

Inhumanity

We marched and reached the highway leading toward Dresden but were rerouted to side roads. After we bypassed Weimar we were the targets of an American air raid. It was interesting that the guards sought protection among us, believing that the pilots, seeing our striped uniforms, would not attack. In the middle of the day we rested in an open field, and food was distributed - a loaf of bread to eight prisoners. In the evening around 10 P.M. we were ordered to stop at a village and were pushed into barns, which became filled beyond capacity. One corner of the barn became the toilet. We noticed that the barn contained bags filled with wheat, oats, potatoes, and beets. We filled our pockets. The SS heard noise coming from inside the barns and opened the doors. They shot inside and killed some prisoners. In the morning the guards came out of the farmer's house, well fed and rested, ready to resume their work of beating and torturing us.

I was in a group of seven who shared similar intellectual interests and stuck together. We shared any extra bread that came our way. On the sixth day, one of us, Robert Garden, could barely drag his feet. With tears in his eyes, he said good-bye in a quiet voice and wished us success in reaching liberation. He said, "I don't know what awaits me, but that is my destiny." We assured him that we would help, but he replied that we should not use up our strength carrying him. When the column started to move he remained sitting with his eyes cast downward to avoid looking at us. We never saw him again.

We made our way through Bad-Berka and then to Sohl-Thal. The guards amused themselves by instigating the dogs on those prisoners too weak to continue. The dogs bit the weak prisoners until they fell. Then they were loaded onto a special vehicle, stacked one upon another. They could not protest anymore.

On the fourth day the rations were reduced to a loaf of bread for twenty prisoners. The next three days there was no food at all. We lived on the raw potatoes and grain we had managed to put in our pockets. For water we had to drink from the street gutters, risking our lives. Some of us contracted diarrhea and died within a day or two. The guards forbade us from drinking the water from the gutters, threatening to shoot anyone caught doing so. On the ninth day we passed the city of Ziegenheim near Bad-Blankenberg. The local German population stood in front of their homes, their eyes down but observing us curiously, nevertheless. The women shook their heads, yet none of them offered us a piece of bread.

Sunday we rested. We counted the minutes, impatiently waiting for the hot potatoes we had been promised. We spoke of nothing but the food-- how we would divide it. Should we eat the potatoes all at once or leave some for the next day? In the evening the guards opened the barn, and we poured out to form a line. Since we were not as fast as they expected, they beat us with their rifle butts and clubs. A young boy tried to advance to the front of the line but was seen by an SS guard. The guard placed his gun in the boy's mouth and shot him, killing him instantly. We froze at this atrocity but only for a second, because our minds were on the potatoes.

We passed the cities of Ziegenruck and Schauenstein and around 10 A.M. we reached Munchberg. The city was in an uproar. A guard asked a local resident what it was all about. The resident answered that the Americans were only three kilometers away. The guard then relayed this news to the other guards.

A few courageous prisoners escaped by mingling with the local population. More of us looked for an opportunity to escape. We reached a farm and stopped at a large barn again. We received our three or four potatoes together with a blow from the guards' club if we didn't move fast enough. We ran up to the top of the barn to eat. When we were ready to leave, the guards noticed that some of us were missing. A local German woman came to complain that some Jews were hiding in her cellar. Two Ukrainian guards and a Romanian ethnic German pounced on the escapees, beat them mercilessly, and then shot them. The head guard pointed out that this would be the fate of anyone else attempting escape.

Our march continued and we reached a forest and then the city of Marktredewitz, which was on the road to the camp of Flossenburg. We passed an old prewar Jewish cemetery, and some prisoners sighed, wishing for a similar burial place when they died. The road wound upwards and seemed endless. They didn't lead us into the camp but ordered us to rest in a large meadow. Most of us fell asleep immediately. The SS amused themselves by throwing pieces of bread at us to watch the prisoners fighting over it. Again we marched all night.

Sixteen days passed in this way. Starvation was the greatest problem. In my small group, only four of the original seven remained. On a Sunday we rested in a barn and there found some pork meat. We ate it. In the meantime the farmer remembered that he had left it there and came running into the barn. We all had to leave the barn and were searched. Somebody who still had a piece of uneaten meat threw it under the feet of our friend Shugal. The SS vultures beat him mercilessly and then set the dogs on him. The dogs ripped the flesh from his body. The guards then poured water over him and continued beating him. As punishment our whole group had to spend the night outdoors in the pouring rain. In the morning we were transferred to an empty factory loft. Shugal, no longer able to walk, was on the wagon for the disabled.

Around midnight we resumed marching. The group seemed smaller. Many were missing. With the rain, hunger and cold, we figured we could last only a few more days. In the evening we were pressed again into a barn full of straw. Because our numbers had shrunk, this time there was sufficient room. The next morning eighteen prisoners were missing. The dogs sniffed them out and they were found. They were assigned to pull the wagon of the disabled. At the outskirts of the village where the forest began, the eighteen prisoners who had tried to escape were ordered to dig a large hole and line up around it. The head Nazi guard then made a speech warning that anyone trying to escape would meet the same fate. He ended his speech with an order to shoot the eighteen prisoners. They all fell into the grave. One of them, a German Jew, turned around to the murderers and shouted, "Revenge will come!" After a few minutes, the hole was filled in with soil, made to appear as before, and the column resumed its march.

Another friend, Harry Blechman tried to slip out of line when he saw an unplowed potato across the road, near a furrow. He was shot and his body left on the side of the road. We were overcome by depression and silence reigned. Our faces were bare bones. Our eyes were like red burning holes, our hair matted down with mud and full of lice. Thus we entered the city of Nemberg am Walde. Its residents were not surprised by our arrival. They were preoccupied with digging antitank holes. They worked diligently to save the Fatherland.

One old German, with his shovel in his hand, turned to one of our guards, saying sarcastically, "We old apes are Hitler's new miracle weapon."

Death March To Buchenwald

Even we smiled hearing the old man saying this. It meant to us that the end was not too far. As we left the city and came toward a village, we heard an exchange of fire. Some peasants came toward the road and warned the SS commander. He immediately ordered us to follow him and his horse-drawn wagon into the forest. The Ukrainians guards killed those who couldn't keep up with their rifle butts, smashing their heads. We walked for a couple of hours and then were ordered to lie down on our stomachs and remain silent. Airplanes swooping down and attacking a truck convoy interrupted the silence. As it became darker, we resumed marching. Somehow we lost my friend, Ingenieur Gindin. We spotted him lying on the asphalt, unable to move. Somebody was pulling off his boots. Another prisoner was removing his blanket. Now there remained only Marcuse and me. We were so exhausted that we were thinking of escaping. The guards kept hurrying us to march faster. We just couldn't and started to shout all together, "We want to rest. We want to eat." At first the guard leader paid no attention, but when the shouting was repeated, the SS head promised a rest at the next village we reached.

In the evening we reached Reichenbach. Peasants came out to see us. Some of the more daring prisoners now disappeared. We stopped there, but as soon as the guards replenished their food supplies we were forced to continue, marching all night long. In the morning the SS commander noticed that many of the prisoners were missing, gone during the night. He scolded the guards but they didn't seem to care very much. Some of them, seeing the end was near, left their weapons and disappeared. Now we were only about three hundred and twenty prisoners, marching past Regensburg, near the Danube River. We were again led into a forest, and we could see the SS commander talking with the guards and pointing at us.

The brutal pace of marching continued day after day. We passed Malersdorf, Landshut, and Munich, and even went past Dachau. Fewer and fewer of us were able to keep the pace as we came into the mountains of Tyrol. Behind us was the U.S. army. It finally caught up with us on May 9 near Einving, close to the city of Salzburg. There remained of the Buchenwald group only one hundred and twenty-eight prisoners out of one thousand six hundred and fifty.

Chapter 22~
The Children, Their Rescuers

A barely mentioned aspect of importance in the history of the Holocaust is the role played by German leftists in rescuing the Jewish children of Buchenwald. In April 1945, the underground, comprised of Socialists, Communists, and other German antifascists, were unwilling to obey the Nazi order to evacuate the Jews. On the advice of the underground, the Jewish children of the two blocks, that housed them, did not report to the gate. The underground instructed the children to remove their Jewish insignia and stay alert. Acts of solidarity like these had a tremendously uplifting effect on the Jewish prisoners. We became aware of "other" Germans besides the Nazis.

Among the German underground leaders who actively worked to save Jews by falsifying personal identification records in the camp office, changing them from Jewish to non-Jewish were Albert Kuntz, later executed by the Nazis, and Robert Sievert and Willy Seifert, both of whom survived and were later active in the government of the DDR. Of particular importance was Hans Eiden, the top prisoner official, who was directly responsible to the Nazis for carrying out all orders within the camp. Wilhelm Hamman, a German Communist who was in charge of the children's block, would be honored in Yad Vashem. He ordered the children not to answer when the SS guards entered the block and asked who was Jewish. He told the Nazi officers that there were no Jewish children in his block.

Death March To Buchenwald

Among the liberated prisoners were close to one thousand Jewish children. This constituted the largest group of Jewish children who survived in Nazi-occupied Europe. They were the remnants of the one and a half million Jewish children who perished.

One of the children saved that day in Buchenwald later became the chief Ashkenazi rabbi of Israel, Meir Lau. Another was the Nobel Prize-winning author, Eli Wiesel.

The children of Buchenwald survived because the prisoner underground, led by Socialists and Communists, resisted the Nazi evacuation orders. Compliance with those orders would have meant certain death for children. Yet some Jewish historians of the Holocaust omit these events. The members of the underground were driven by the ideals of socialism and humanism.

In museums in New York, Washington, DC, Jerusalem, and elsewhere, which have been built to remember the Holocaust, this underground should be honored, not just as individuals but also as a collective. If we, who have lived through the Holocaust, are to retain our integrity, indeed our souls, such an acknowledgement must not be avoided. This historical credit is long overdue.

Chapter 23- Conclusion

The French government offered to take in as residents a few hundred of the children from Buchenwald. I was among a few adults chosen to accompany them. Our rehabilitation into normal life was undertaken by the French-Jewish philanthropic organization Oeuvre de Secure des Enfants (OSE). We were sent to various cities in France, where we were housed in dormitories and provided with basic necessities, as well as some form of education. A few months passed, and I was in Paris when I began to attend meetings of a society (Landsmanshaft) of former Bendzin Jews who had immigrated to France before the war. There I met some survivors of other camps who had made their way into France on their own. One of them had just returned from a sanatorium located in the Pyrenees. He told me he had met other Bendziners there.

When I asked him if he had met a young woman named Nitzah, to my great joy he replied yes. I was perplexed as to how she had come to France after liberation. With her Aryan identity papers, I had assumed that she had a better chance than other Jews to survive the war. I was eager to confirm if this was indeed my Nitzah. I sent a telegram, reading, "Nitzah, I am alive! I am in Paris with the OSE." The next day I received a reply from her, stating that she was coming to see me immediately. And thus we were reunited.

This is what had happened to Nitzah after her last visit to me in Cobelwitz,

"The mayor of Cosel had told me that if I was not pleased with my job at the baker's, he would find me another one. Later, after I quarreled with the baker, I took the mayor up on his offer. He found me a job in a paper factory. There were other Polish workers there. Luckily I passed a test to work in the laboratory where only Germans worked. This meant that, at least during the day, I was not exposed to the Poles who might have guessed my Jewish identity, since I spoke Polish with a Jewish accent. Perhaps some of them suspected, but they did not betray me.

I remained in the paper factory until the German army began to retreat. Then the foreign workers in Cosel were evacuated to Czechoslovakia, where we were finally liberated by American soldiers. I approached an American soldier and asked to be sent to where there were other Jews. He called over another soldier who spoke to me in Yiddish. To my utter amazement, when I tried to respond, I could not say a word in Yiddish. My fear of murmuring it in my sleep had pushed it into the far recesses of my brain. It was several weeks before I was able to speak it again. After the war I assumed that Jochanan had perished with all the others."

In Paris Nitzah informed me that her sister Esther was the sole survivor of her immediate family and that she was living in Regensburg, Germany. We decided to join her there and plan our immigration to Israel. However, due to the fact that Nitzah had several aunts and uncles in the U.S., who had immigrated there before the war, we changed our mind and applied for visas to the U.S. While we waited in Regensburg, we got married, and two years later my wife gave birth to our daughter. Three months later we were on a plane to New York City, where we have lived ever since.

Part of Old Bendzin with the synagogue and castle, the symbol of the city.

THE LAST JEWS OF BENDZIN: 1939-1944

PREFACE TO 1st EDITION

The book contains the history and fate of the Jewish population of the City of Bendzin during the five years of Nazi-rule 1939-1944.

The following pages are based on my experience and partly related to me by my few surviving friends. I wish to honor my friend Toviah Kaminsky, member of the underground group for his help in remembering events and places.

Let the following pages be a living monument to the youth of Bendzin among whom I lived and loved and to whom this book is devoted.

The Author

CHAPTER I - LIFE UNTIL 1939

The old town of Bendzin is located in the south central part of Poland, in the province of Katowice. It is part of an industrial area known as Upper Silesia or Zaglembie, which is famous for its coalmines and iron plants.

In 1939 there were about 35,000 Jews in the town, making up 70% of the total population and representing a wide range of occupations. In Polish Catholic society class differences were sharply defined, and a similar structure could be observed among the Jewish population. This was especially true after World War I, when a large part of the impoverished middle class became proletarian. Bendzin therefore had a considerable Jewish working class, not only in the needle and leather trades, but in the factories of heavy industry as well. Transport and communication had been Jewish trades for centuries. However, the majority of the Jewish population, consisted of small business people and independent artisans.

The community also had its capitalists. The two richest men were Firstenberg, who employed seven thousand people in his zinc plant, and Yankiel Guttman, who was in iron manufacturing. Both were active philanthropists, and there were no charitable institutions in the town they had not helped to fund. Yankiel Guttman had given many young chalutzim (Hebrew word for pioneers) their fares to Israel and many poor brides their dowries. And shortly before World War II, an ultra-modern orphanage was built in the town, thanks chiefly to the money and initiative of these two men. There were not many others in their class like them.

The Jewish population of Bendzin, which dated from the time the town was founded in the 11th century, was the leading Jewish community of Upper Silesia. The whole Jewish population of the province was estimated at around 120,000 and, outside of Bendzin, Jews made up only a small minority in any of the towns and villages where they lived. The only two Yiddish newspapers published in the province were published in Bendzin, and the political parties all had their strongest regional organizations there. There were also several Yiddish libraries, a Yiddish theatre and the musical groups "Hazamir" and "Muse". There were Yeshivot (religious schools), elementary schools like Yavneh, and a Hebrew gymnasium or high school. Yiddish was spoken by everyone, from the laborer to the professional man, and Jewish secular life flourished. The Jewish population was aware of and responsive to everything that befell the Jewish people throughout the world. In short, Bendzin was the social, cultural and political center of Jewish life in the province.

The greatest treasure Bendzin's Jewry possessed was its youth. Revolutionary, yet absolutely committed to their Jewish identity, full of life and energy, they were trying to solve the problems of their people and were ready to make any sacrifice to do so - as was later proved in the time of hunger, enslavement and extermination.

The majority of the young people belonged to youth movements or sports clubs, which represented every political shade - those who were not part of any organization had very little influence. Like their elders, most of the young Jews of the province were Zionists and about eighty or ninety per cent of their clubs had this orientation. However, there were also non-Zionist groups like the Bund, the Communists, or the extremely religious Poale-Agudat Israel.

Unlike Diaspora Judaism of the present, which must struggle for its very existence, Jewish life in prewar Bendzin flourished. And the rising generation gave every promise that it would continue to do so.

Just before the outbreak of the war, Mordechai Ber Rosenberg, a Zionist labor leader, published a town almanac, chronicling almost a millennium of Jewish life in the town.

So it was for years. Then came the autumn of 1939.

CHAPTER II- THE FIRST PERIOD OF THE GERMAN REICH

September 1, 1939 - December 31, 1940

The Nazis Are Coming

On Friday, September 1, 1939, Hitler's hordes marched across the border into Poland, thus beginning the Second World War.

On the afternoon of that day 70 young men and women, members of Kibbutz Borochov, a commune, met to discuss what to do. Should they leave town or not?

Although fighting had already broken out in a few places, many people were still reluctant to believe that the war had in fact begun. Two kibbutz members argued that there had already been several occasions on which the war seemed to have started, and each time it turned out to be a false alarm. They believed the present scare was merely another such case. Hitler, they claimed, wouldn't dare to attack Poland. The man in the street was even more skeptical of the reality of the war.

Nevertheless, the majority voted to pack up and evacuate immediately so as not to fall into the hands of the Nazis. Once packed, however, we waited, still hoping for an announcement that the war had not begun after all and that the situation could once more be considered normal.

But that night the first refugees came streaming through the town: people on foot carrying bundles, others riding on vans, farmers leading cows. By morning the roads were filled with thousands of people trying to outdistance the enemy. The kibbutz hesitated no longer; it piled its provisions onto a van and joined the exodus. The day before no one had dreamed of leaving. Today, at the sight of those thousands of marchers, panic broke out. Most of the Jewish population left the town.

On Monday the Nazis arrived in a motorized column that passed through the heart of the city. No one dared step out onto the streets. Motors roaring, the column circled the town a few times in a show of strength designed to inspire fear in the hearts of the townspeople. The dust on their long leather coats suggested they had already been in the field for several days and their silent faces boded no good. After completing their circuit of the city they drove on, leaving a commandant and his staff in charge of the town.

Strange as it may seem our neighbors, the Poles, did not appear to feel affected by the new order. For them it was merely another change of government, and they tried to go along with it. They gave no sign of mourning over their lost independence, if indeed they had ever known they possessed it. Only an occasional intelligent individual showed that he realized what had happened to his country.

The Germans advanced through the country so quickly that they were able to trap thousands of refugees in their flight. Coming home, many of these Jews found their homes looted. The lower elements among their neighbors, anticipating a German pogrom, had been looking forward to an opportunity to plunder Jewish homes. However, as it happened, the Nazis beat them to it.

One of the first results of the invasion was that it became difficult to buy food. Bread was particularly scarce and people had to get on line outside bakeries as early as four or five in the morning and wait until they opened. It often happened that a German policeman would come along, pick out whatever Jews he noticed in the line and chase them away. When satisfied that he had gotten them all he would turn to go, only to be stopped by some Poles in the line, who were always ready to point out the few extra Jews who had escaped detection because of their non-Jewish appearance. Pleased with such "cooperation", the Nazi would take the unfortunates away, and beat them up. The crowd, now "Jew-free" would often laugh with satisfaction.

Confiscations and Extortions

The office of the local commandant soon began taking an official interest in the Jews - that is, it began to demand money from them. In time each official of this local government found his way to the leaders of the Jewish community and asked for money, "otherwise..." The sentence was never finished, but we knew what was meant. A few more Jews would be shot for fun. One of the largest of these extortions deserves special mention. The Gestapo ordered it in February 1940.

E. Weinzieher, the head of the Jewish community at that time, summoned the most prominent Jewish leaders of the town to a meeting in the rooms of the kibbutz and read the Gestapo order to them. "By four o'clock tomorrow the Jews of Bendzin shall hand over to the authorities 15 kilograms (about 35 pounds) of gold and 60 kilograms (about 135 pounds) of silver. Otherwise, harsh measures will be taken." "Harsh measures" was a blanket threat implying persecutions, shootings, etc.

Weinzieher begged his listeners to make every possible effort to raise the amount needed to avoid catastrophe. Already the synagogue had been burnt down and forty Jews shot to death in a single day. So for one day selected pairs of people went around the city asking everyone for whatever precious metal they might possess. Jews gave up their most treasured belongings, even their wedding rings, in an effort to save the town from further bloodshed. The next day the community leaders delivered the tribute. The gold was about two pounds short of the required amount, but there were forty extra pounds of silver.

About two weeks after this it was announced that all Jews were to bring their radios to Police Station B and from that time on, they would be forbidden to own any. The Polish population had to follow suit a few weeks later. Three weeks after this the Gestapo ordered the delivery of all skiing equipment: shoes, socks, clothes, etc.

In addition to all this the Germans were in the daily habit of walking into Jewish homes and taking whatever they wanted. Often a Nazi would walk into a house that had caught his eye and order everyone in it to leave within five minutes, taking nothing with them. He would then move his family into the house. This usually happened to richer people. Weeping, they took leave of their homes.

During the winter of 1941 the Germans announced that the Jews had to deliver all their fur coats to the authorities, with no exceptions being made for women and children. Anyone found with a piece of fur in his house would be severely punished. The Germans acquired thousands of furs as a result of this maneuver, and our "good neighbors" profited nicely as well. To avoid delivering their coats to the Nazis, many people tried to sell them instead to their Polish neighbors. Since this had to be done within one or two days, the pieces were sold for a fraction of their true value.

Another confiscation involved all electrical appliances, from the smallest to the most complicated. The penalty for disobeying this order was death.

Week after week there came new laws, looting and despoiling the Jews of the province. Every Jewish business was put under the control of a German, called Treuhanderstelle, or trustee, who was to administer it until a German could be found to buy it. Until then, the business belonged to the Treuhandstelle, a branch of the Nazi Party. Usually the Jewish owner was thrown out after a week or two, but in some cases, where the business was more complicated, he would be kept on until he had taught his expropriators how to run it, and then let go.

Next came a series of restrictive laws. Jews were no longer allowed to use the main streets of the town. Any Jew still living on one had to build a special exit in the back of his house. As time went on more and more streets were forbidden to Jews, so that a ghetto of sorts was gradually established. Jews were not allowed to enter the town's parks and squares, including a certain well-known grassy hill located in the Jewish section.

Swimming in the river or resting near it was also forbidden. Anyone caught doing either was beaten or drowned.

Jews were forbidden to use the railroad. A Jew wanting to go to a nearby town would have to get special permission to do so, and even then he would have to ride on the platform.

Armbands and Law Enforcement

When the Nazi occupation was two months old, all Jews were ordered to wear a white armband with a Star of David on it. The punishment for not obeying was severe. People without a band were the first to be sent to Auschwitz. After a while this order was replaced by a new one: every Jew over the age of ten had to wear two yellow Jewish stars, one in front and one in back. The Nazis often went through the streets, hunting for Jews not wearing the star. When these expeditions failed to bring in enough victims, they extended their area of search to houses and apartments, although the law stated that the star was only to be worn in the streets. The people collected in this manner were beaten, tortured and forced to do the hardest work. After that, we wore our armbands and later our badges everywhere, no matter what the law said.

The individual German policeman had unlimited power. The penalty for jaywalking, for example, was either a fine of one mark (about 50 cents) or deportation to Auschwitz. It depended entirely on the mood of the policeman involved. If he were willing to do so, he would accept the fine. If he was not, he wrote down the "lawbreaker's" name and address, and some time later the police would come for him at night and take him away to the death camp. The luckiest people were those who never had to go out at all.

Going to Russia

Once they lived through the first month, most people realized that the Nazi occupation could only end tragically. At about the same time letters began to arrive from Russian-occupied Poland, saying that Jews there still lived in freedom and security. This information made a strong impression on the town's young people, many of who packed their knapsacks and left for Russia. The letters they sent back from the east were encouraging, and increasing numbers of their friends followed them.

Going to Russia or "crossing the San" became the most popular topic of conversation of the day. The San River was the boundary between German and Russian Poland. It flowed through the town of Przemysl, which it divided into a German and a Russian sector. People arriving there had to wait until dark to cross or ford the river, as both Germans and Russians would shoot anyone they caught trying to get across. People often had had to make as many as three separate attempts to cross the river before it was safe to proceed. Even so, a considerable part of Bendzin's youth immigrated to Russian territory.

As described before, the members of Kibbutz Borochov had already tried to escape the Nazis once by leaving town when the war broke out. Now the San River project presented the idea of escape for a second time. Far into the night, the kibbutz members debated whether to go or stay. Of its two leading members, one, Moshe Margolis, was in favor of leaving. The other, Hershl Springer, wanted to stay. The group that wanted to leave argued that the kibbutz had no chance of surviving if it remained in Nazi territory. Their opponents, who were in the minority, said that as long as there were young Jews in Bendzin, they should stay. They pointed out that there were even kibbutzim in Germany. (There had even been some limited emigration from these places to Israel before the war began.)

The final decision was that the great majority who wanted to leave for Russian territory should do so. The minority was not obligated to go along with them. No one wanted to assume that much responsibility. When the departures began, many families from the town joined in, as conditions were still very bad. A number of youth organizations also decided to go. Only nine members of Kibbutz Borochov were left in town.

As time went on, however, we began to get word that crossing the border was becoming more and more difficult. As larger numbers of people gathered at the frontier, the Russians put more soldiers on guard to prevent them from crossing over. On the other side the Germans robbed the refugees bare. They also began to seize them in large numbers and send them to Krakow for internment in forced-labor camps. All this brought about a reduction in the rate of emigration. At the same time, life in the province was gradually beginning to get better. The Jews were given food ration cards. The Germans strengthened the authority of the Judenrat, which took over the administration of the Jewish community. People began to work and earn money on a regular basis, and the terrifying random shootings stopped. This improvement in our living conditions was the main reason why emigration largely came to an end.

Jews were optimistic about the future now. "They need our work in the factories, so they have to feed us and let us live," the reasoning went. "After all, how much longer can the war last?" The general belief was that we had only a few more months to suffer. Everyone was convinced that the war would be over and the Nazis defeated inside of six months. This was in 1940.

The Kibbutz

The group of young people who made up Kibbutz Borochov played an important role in Bendzin's community life. During the Nazi occupation they did their share in the glorious work of the Jewish Resistance in Poland.

There were hundreds of kibbutzim in pre-war Poland. They were part of a movement to train young chalutzim, for life in Israel by having them live and work together in collective groups. Bendzin's Kibbutz Borochov was founded in 1936. It was named after one of the leaders and theoreticians of the Socialist Zionist movement, Ber Borochov, who died at an early age in Russia in 1917.

In the beginning, the kibbutz was located in some apartments in a suburb of the town, where twenty or thirty people lived in one room in very poor conditions. After a few years of hard work, the kibbutz members were able to leave their cramped quarters and move to a more comfortable location at 30 Kolontaja Street in town, where they could accommodate many new members.

At the time people in the Jewish community couldn't understand the boy with unkempt hair and patched trousers, or a girl in army boots who didn't want to eat with her boss. Anti-Zionist labor groups spread the rumor that people from the kibbutz were working for lower wages, which was of course untrue. Some who knew better than to believe that rumor, nevertheless shook their heads sadly over these young people, who came for the most part from good homes. Those members who had come from other towns were quite unpopular - after all, they were strangers. In 1939 a young friend told me that when he first came to Bendzin and asked a man how to get to the kibbutz, the man, who was a religious Jew, looked at him pityingly and asked, "Are people still going to the kibbutz?" The younger man's dismay at this reaction soon evaporated in the tumultuous welcome with which the kibbutz greeted every newcomer. Nevertheless this episode does serve to illustrate the average person's attitude toward the kibbutz at that time.

In spite of everything the kibbutz persevered and continued to prepare young pioneers for life in Israel, giving them a thorough grounding in the tenets of socialism and Zionism. In its new apartment on Kolontaja Street it soon grew to two hundred members. The illegal emigrations to Israel which occurred during 1938 and 1939 had almost emptied it completely, but by the time the war began membership was back up to about seventy.

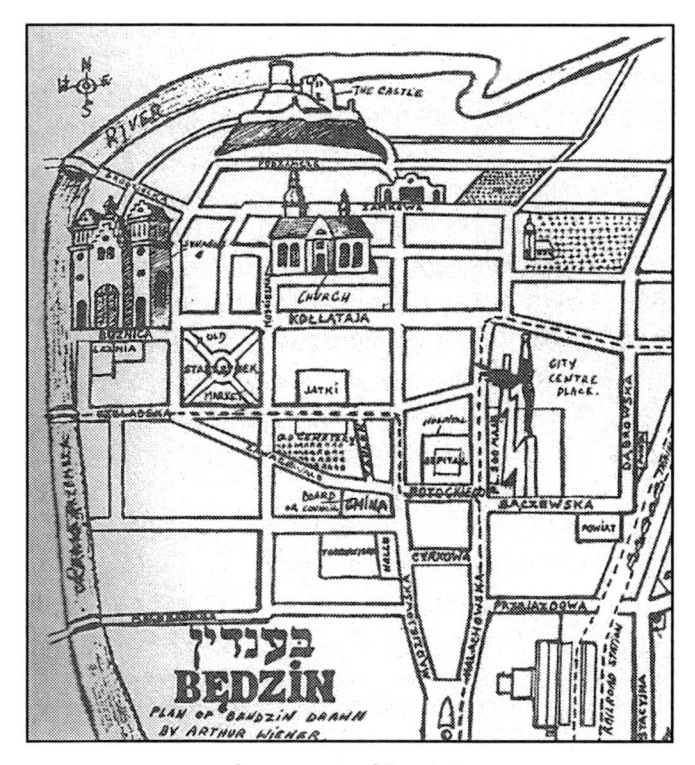

Street map of Bendzin

In 1938, when anti-Semitism had begun to take the form of semi-official boycotts and pogroms such as the one in Przytyk, which had the blessing of the Polish government and the participation of the police, Bendzin was ready. Our kibbutz, like its counterparts in other towns all over Poland, was the backbone and nerve center of the self-defense organization. Later, after the Nazi invasion, the town's youth gathered ever more closely around the kibbutz. The ideological differences between the different groups became less important as people sought a feeling of warmth and solidarity in the face of a common enemy. In addition, the Jewish community of the town had lost all contact with Warsaw. The Polish capital, which had the largest Jewish population of any city in the country, was also the national headquarters for all Jewish political and cultural groups. All contact that Bendzin had with the outside world was now in the hands of the kibbutz.

CHAPTER III- THE SOCIAL AND POLITICAL LIFE OF THE TOWN'S YOUTH

January 1, 1941 - December 8, 1942

The Factories

One of the most important factors in creating community life for the young people of the town was the normalization of living conditions that took place once the Nazis began using the Jews as a source of cheap labor. There was political activity among the town's youth as early as the summer of 1940, when living conditions were still extremely difficult and chaotic. But now that a small measure of economic improvement for the Jews seemed assured, it became possible for the first time to speak of a real social and cultural life for the young Jews of Bendzin.

For one thing, Alfred Rosner's shop was established. Rosner, a German, had come to Bendzin with nothing and built a shop with machines confiscated from the Jews. The shop grew into a factory where seven thousand men and women manufactured uniforms for the Werhmacht, the German Army.

After Rosner another German came, Michatz, who set up a shop employing one thousand people. A few other Germans established shoe factories. The latter did not actually create anything new, however; they merely expropriated a string of small businesses and joined them together.

The machinery was stolen, the labor forced. For the German entrepreneurs, manpower was plentiful and cheap. For the Jewish laborers, a certificate of employment meant that its bearer was safe from the possibility of deportation to a slave-labor camp.

A certain number of Jewish employees began to return to work in stores that had once been owned by Jews. No matter how small the salary was, it still meant the difference between life and death.

The Youth Groups and the Moazah

With the return of something like normal living and working conditions, the youth groups began to resume their work, even though membership in such organizations was punishable by death. Officially it was only meetings of ten people or more that were forbidden, but for the Germans six or seven people together were enough to arouse suspicion.

The first to organize were the youth movements of the Labor Zionist parties, such as Dror, a socialist Zionist group, Gordonia, the youth group of the right wing Socialists Zionists, and Hashomer Hatzair, "The Young Guard", a leftwing Zionist organization. A little later they were joined by Hanoar Hatzioni, or "Zionist Youth", a rightwing group with a substantial membership. Still later came Hashomer Hadati, "The Religious Guard", made up of religious Zionists, the Poale-Zion's leftwing youth group, and finally the Communists. These groups held their first meetings in the strictest secrecy in people's apartments or in the kibbutz. Their goal was to bring the young people of the community to a full understanding of what was going on.

The Last Jews of Bendzin

*A group of members of the Sports organization
Hapoel in Bendzin*

Once organized, these groups created a central body, called the Moazah, to which each organization sent two representatives. It should be mentioned that the kibbutz played a major role in forming this umbrella group. Its leader, Hershl Springer, had the gift of winning people's confidence and persuading them to agree to compromise when necessary. Two groups, which nevertheless did not come in, were Poale Zion and Betar. Betar, an extreme rightwing group, didn't show much life outside of their annual Jabotinski Memorials, they were too small a group to carry much weight in town. Poale Zion Left, later became active when self-defense was being organized.

The active core of each group consisted of the most committed and idealistic members, whose involvement with the movement dated from before the start of the war. In Hanoar Hatzioni such people included Israel Diamond, Carola Baum* Arie Hasenberg, Kerner and Borzykowski. The leaders of Hashomer-Hadati were Shlomo Ehrlich, Aaron Feldberg* and Nathan Shiff. In Hashomer Hatzair the most active members were

*immigrated to Israel after the war

David Koslowski, Chaika Klinger*, Nadzia Klugman and, never to be forgotten, the Pesachson sisters.

Adek Grunwald, A. Fishl* and Itzchak Grinbaum were the leading members of Dror, and in Gordonia the central figures were: Hanka Borenstein, Schlomo Zimmerman, Shlomo Lerner, Motek Krzesivo* and Kalman Blacharz*.

These boys and girls were the best that youth anywhere could produce, full of energy, intelligence and the qualities necessary for social leadership. They never shrank from any sacrifice for the Jewish people that might be required of them. In their humanitarian ideals and the clarity of their moral vision they could be compared to those legendary heroes of the Russian liberation movement, the Narodnaia Vola (the "People's Will"), and in fact the youth activists of our town had grown up with those Russian fighters as an ideal. Borzykowski's book Flames, which tells about the history and struggles of the Narodnaia Vola, was the most popular book in town during the war. It became an inspiration for the many young people who read it.

Meanwhile the Moazah had contacted Nathan Shwalbe, who worked for HeChalutz in Switzerland. Shwalbe began sending bulletins to Bendzin, which ostensibly consisted of information about vacations. In reality they contained news from Palestine and other parts of the world. Later the kibbutz and the youth movements received food packages, which were given to comrades in need.

We also established a connection of sorts with our sister movements in Berlin and Vienna. From the latter we had a visitor, Aaron Mentzer, the director of Youth Aliyah (Hebrew for immigration to Israel.) It was encouraging to learn that the Zionist movement was active even in the heart of Nazi Germany.

As time went on the amount of youth activity in the town increased. Young people who had been unattached joined up and new organizations were formed. The cells worked to capacity teaching their members the basics of Socialism, Zionism, and Jewish history, all of which were studied more seriously than they would have been in normal times.

*immigrated to Israel after the war

The Last Jews of Bendzin

These groups offered their members a substitute for school. There was a healthy, home-like atmosphere with friendly instructors, who were more like older brothers.

In the early spring of 1942 the Moazah took a census of the organized groups in Bendzin.

The results were as follows:

Hanoar Hatzioni	500 members
Gordonia	300 members
Dror	250 members
Hashomer Hatzair	200 members
Hashomer Hadati	150 members

The others generally knew the size of each group since the leaders of one organization would often take part in the meetings of another. Kibbutz members in particular were invited to the larger assemblies. It should also be mentioned that the size of a group did not necessarily determine its effectiveness. Hashomer Hatzair and Dror, although smaller than some of the others, had extremely energetic organizers.

Each group had its own personality. The majority of Hashomer Hatzair were girls who worked for the movement with all their hearts - whereas some of the rightwing organizations took their task less seriously. Another characteristic of the groups was that about half their members were children between the ages of ten (the minimum required for admission) and fourteen. Later on, when the deportations to Auschwitz began and greater risks were taken, this younger element was excluded.

The Judenrat

Moniek Merin, the man named by a high Gestapo official to be chairman of the district Judenrat, or Jewish council, had been a notorious gambler before the war (though also a nominal member of the General Zionist Party). Now, in a post that made him the official "representative" of the Jewish community of Upper Silesia, he had the power of life and death over every Jew in the province. He kept this position by continually bribing the Gestapo chiefs with money and gifts. He was the one to decide who would be in charge of the smaller local councils, which had been established in each city. In Bendzin, his choice for the post was a man named Molczadski who had won his favor with his organizational skills and his blind obedience.

Molczadski had been a member of Poale Zion before the war and claimed to be a good Labor Zionist still. The party, however, no longer recognized him as a member, stating that he had had no right to accept such a position without their permission. He tried to keep in the party's good graces nevertheless by maintaining contact with former members and dispensing favors to the better-known personalities. Claiming to be a loyal party man, he insisted that everything he was doing was for the good of the community. He wanted to have an excuse for after the war.

Later it became evident that he was a traitor to his people. When the youth groups were trying to set up an organization for self-defense, he dismissed the idea as unnecessary and added that, if it should eventually be required, he would be the one to take care of it. He was referring to the small, unarmed group of men who made up the Jewish militia or police. Too corrupt and cowardly to risk their lives in an illegal defense, they came mostly from the lowest elements of society.

Molczadski showed his true colors again at the very end when the ghetto was being wiped out. It became clear then that his only objective was that he should be the last to go, no matter how many thousands of people had to precede him into the gas chambers. This was at the time that the young fighters of Bendzin were making their last stand against the Nazi beast in the bunkers, fighting to the last man and saving the honor of Bendzin's Jews.

The activities of the youth groups got a considerable boost when the farm was established. Situated about two and a half miles from town in the village of Srodula-Dolna, or Lower Srodula, it quickly became the chief meeting place for the young people of the area. It should be remembered that political meetings were prohibited in town, and that the kibbutz was particularly likely to be suspected by the Germans of having violated this rule. Officially, of course, the kibbutz was nothing more than a group of laborers living together and working in the laundry, (the only mechanized one in town) which they had originally owned but had later signed over to the Judenrat, fearing confiscation.

The farm was established in the spring of 1941 on land originally belonging to a confiscated Polish coalmine corporation. About one square mile in size, it had previously been divided into small lots. It was offered to the Judenrat by the German district inspector for agriculture, who bore the responsibility for all the farming done in the area. For the Judenrat it was largely an unwanted responsibility until the Moazah came along and suggested turning it into a combination farm and agricultural school. What they really envisioned was a farming kibbutz. The Judenrat agreed and was promised all the profits that the project might bring.

Kibbutz Borochov sent its ten best members to organize the work. Each youth group followed suit with a work force of ten or more, and so it began. In the beginning it was difficult. Over a hundred boys and girls worked in the field, struggling with soil that hadn't been cultivated for a number of years. At night they had to go home to their parents, as their living quarters were not yet completed. They were sustained by the knowledge that the work they were doing was important and that as the elite of their organizations they had to set an example for the others.

In time young people came to the farm to socialize, not only from Bendzin but by stealth, from the neighboring towns of Sosnowitz and Dombova as well. Every Saturday afternoon the roads to the village were filled with young people walking, talking and meeting their friends. Meetings, lectures and classes were held in the fields and dormitories. On Saturday evenings there were cultural programs with dramatic presentations and folk dancing far into the night. From these hours together the young people drew the courage and inspiration to continue their work.

The farm soon developed into as important a center of social life as the town. Because so many of the most active young people were now living on it, the farm became a source of organizational and moral support for the town's activities. The youth groups flourished under its influence and their work grew. Among other things, the Moazah undertook an elaborate cultural program.

It should be mentioned in this connection that the Judenrat also tried to do something in the cultural sphere, and a few concerts and theatrical presentations were given under its auspices. The Council, however, was not ultimately responsible for the fact that these performances took place. A group of artists and musicians from the pre-war "Muse", a theatrical, choral and orchestral society, led by Mendel Kaner, had taken the initiative in assembling a dramatic company and orchestra. Kaner was one of the few members of the Judenrat not tainted with corruption. Under his direction the folk chorus gave an excellent performance of some of those Jewish classics concerned with social consciousness and the hope for a better tomorrow, such as Y. L. Peretz's "Don't Think the World is a Tavern."

The officials of the Judenrat barely tolerated this kind of enterprise. Interestingly enough, when the actress Sonia Boczkowska wanted to recite about Jewish poverty and suffering the head of the district council, Merin, forbade it in order not to "sadden" the population. In general the Judenrat had very little interest in cultural activities and didn't try to pretend otherwise. They were just obeying orders.

Schools

The young people ignored the Nazi ban on organizational activity and continued their work. The two years ending with the final destruction of Bendzin's Jewish community in December of 1942 were to prove the most productive period for the youth of the underground, even though conditions on the outside were getting worse all the time. The slave labor camps already existed and about a tenth of our comrades had been sent to them. In addition, every few weeks there were deportations to Auschwitz consisting of people who had been caught while trying to escape from central Poland, now under the control of the Nazis' "General-Government." Those who, fleeing death and starvation, managed to get to our area were often arrested by the Jewish militia, who were acting under Merin's orders.

In spite of these dangers the youth leaders wanted to set up schools for the children, as it was now two years since they had had any proper education. Through letters from the Warsaw Ghetto we had learned that not only were there underground schools there, but a high school as well, under the direction of Yitzchak Zukerman ("Antek"), who had been a HeChalutz leader before the war. (This hero, who was later to be the second-in-command of the revolt of the Warsaw Ghetto, settled in Israel after the war in the Kibbutz of the Ghetto Fighters.) There he directed a museum, the largest private one in the country, dedicated to the memory of the Resistance.)

The Moazah went to work and in a short time hundreds of children between the ages of seven and thirteen were attending schools under its supervision. The aim of these schools was to give both a general and a Jewish education, the latter centering on Israel and the study of Hebrew. Each organization gave its best people, who set about organizing the children into classes and arranging for rooms in which to meet. Soon every street in the neighborhood had a few such improvised classrooms and each teacher a few classes. These teachers - mainly seventeen and eighteen year-old boys and girls - were the heroes of their students, who studied under them eagerly. It became a common occurrence to meet these young men and women in the street as they hurried from one class to the next.

Naturally an enterprise involving so many people and so much space could not be kept a secret from the Judenrat, as the Jewish section was by now quite small and congested. Accordingly, a delegation of teachers went to Molczadski and made their work known to him. He promised them some financial aid to enable the teachers to spend more time with their children, but this did not materialize. The schools never got any help from the Council, but the work went on nevertheless.

The Press

At the same time that the schools were being established, an underground press, which was mostly the work of the youth groups, came into being. The first publication, after Bendzin, to issue from it was under Nazi rule, is particularly worthy of note. It was a two-page pamphlet printed by the left wing of Poale Zion (the Labor Zionists), which sought to reveal the reactionary and traitorous nature of the Judenrat. It warned decent social and political leaders not to associate themselves with the clique whose membership made up the council. The Judenrat, it declared, "is a group of people without any independence blindly obeying the Germans in everything. Their aim is to save their own skins even if the whole community has to be exterminated for it." The authors went further and attacked Moniek Merin, the head of the district council, thus placing themselves in even greater danger. The pamphlet made a strong impression in town as it marked the first attempt to speak out on this situation. Later different youth groups began putting out their own papers but these dealt mainly with ideological issues such as fascism, socialism and Zionism rather than with current political events.

The first such journal to appear was Haboneh (The Builder), which was issued by Dror. Next came Przelom (Breakthrough), written in Polish, the work of Hashomer Hatzair, and then a journal that Hanoar Hatzioni put out under an assumed identity. The farm also issued a bulletin devoted to political problems. It was an open forum in which anyone could express his views. The Stalinist and Trotzkyist papers, which came to us from outside the town, were written in Polish. We also received periodicals from Warsaw representing every point of view along the political spectrum.

Libraries

A few months after the war began the Nazis confiscated all known libraries, taking the books back to the paper mills for shredding. A part of the library belonging to the cultural group known as the Muse was saved by being divided up and hidden in private houses and in the cellar of the orphan home. The kibbutz library, comprising seven hundred volumes, was spared because it was private not public. In the beginning the youth of the town used the kibbutz library, but as time went on the demand for books became so great that the kibbutz could no longer meet it. Once again, the youth organizations stepped in to deal with the problem. Working secretly, Dror installed its library in a private apartment on Podwale St. For reasons of security, it was to be used by members only. Books were brought in by party members, old and young alike, and a large part came from the kibbutz's store of duplicate copies. A few were stolen from the cellar of the orphanage, where reading matter forbidden by the Judenrat was kept. Hanoar Hatzioni and Hashomer Hatzair established libraries of their own, and other groups set up arrangements by which they exchanged their books with one another.

There were also two private libraries in town whose owners made their living by lending their books. It was here that the average Jew found his reading material. One of these was located in the small room in which a Mr. Kestenbaum lived. He was quite an intelligent man and made a successful business of lending books, even though his quarters were so cramped that he had to move his bed outside during the day in order to give his customers room to move around. He owned about six or seven hundred books.

The second lending library belonged to a man named Rosenberg, who was an old member of the Poale Zion's leftwing. He had loved books all his life and spent every cent he could on them, with the result that he had put together a considerable collection. He had books on general science, economics, philosophy, socialism and a number of interesting old periodicals. A serious man, he always tried to encourage readers to choose a serious book rather than a sensational thriller, but there was a great demand for fiction at that time. People wanted to be able to live in the illusion of a better life for at least the few hours they were reading.

The underground journals found their way to any place in the country where Jews lived, even the smallest villages. They were read in secrecy and hidden from the older people, who were afraid of having illegal items around. Liaison men, sent by the Moazah on matters of cooperation between youth groups, brought them. It was difficult work because there was an official order forbidding Jews to travel from one town to another, and so back roads through the fields and woods had to be taken. Buses were also forbidden, and any Jew who tried to ride on one and was discovered would lose his life.

The Seminars

The children's school started by the Moazah was not the only educational project undertaken by the youth groups. With the help of the Kibbutz, Dror set up a seminar for youth leaders. It met in an attic room of the kibbutz's headquarters and lasted eight days, from eight in the morning until nightfall, and was attended by twenty boys and girls from the district. It was an enterprise involving financial hardship as well as personal risk. Each kibbutz member had to divide his already small allotment of food and share it with the students. But the end result was more strength for the movement. Living in a world that had become a slaughterhouse, our young people had a chance to learn about the sources of humane values, which were eternal, by studying history, literature and economy. Among the lecturers were Frumkah Plotnitzkah, a member of the Central Committee of Hechalutz in Warsaw; Hershl Springer, chairman of the kibbutz; and Gedaliah Sobkowski, a well known trade union leader. The elder Bundist, Mr. Pesachson, lectured on the history and problems of the Jewish labor movement.

Since I was so strongly in favor of the idea of a seminar, I was put in charge of the project and asked to do some additional lecturing. Hershl Springer, a former member of Dror, showed his great understanding of the work by helping financially.

Hashomer Hatzair held a similar study group with good results in spite of the considerable difficulties they encountered. Mordecai Anielewicz, later the hero and commander of the Warsaw Uprising, was staying in Bendzin at that time and was also a teacher at this seminar. He spoke with energy and clarity, making a strong impression on all who heard him. With him we stayed up far into the night, talking about politics. He told us about the work going on in the area of the General Government, and about how conditions were worsening everywhere. At the same time he acknowledged and encouraged the work he saw being done in Bendzin.

The Slovakian Hope

In its relations with the town's youth the kibbutz was generally understood to be a sort of older brother, one who could offer guidance and arbitrate disputes, and as such it enjoyed a certain respect in the town. As it happened life within the kibbutz was not always completely harmonious, possibly because so many different kinds of people were represented in it. Nevertheless it was able to carry out its mission of uniting the various outside groups for necessary projects. However, in order to assume this role, the kibbutz had had to undergo certain changes. The nucleus of nine members who had remained after the rest had left for the east could not have done it alone. But in the winter of 1941 something happened that made the kibbutz ripe for its historic task. This was the Slovakian venture, a rescue project that became associated with the Zionist movement. At that time it was a glimmer of light on the horizon, which up till then had been unrelievedly dark. It didn't last long and it ended unhappily - apparently because of one man's jealousy of another who was in a position to help save people from hell. Here is the story.

About forty miles from Bendzin was a small town called Osviecim with a Jewish population of about three thousand, most of who were still there in 1941. As was the Germans' practice in a town of that area which they considered to be part of the Reich, the Nazis changed its name to a Germanized form. The town now was called Auschwitz.

At one end of town they built the concentration camp, which they called "Koncentrations Lager Auschwitz" (K-L Auschwitz.) We had known about the existence of concentration camps since 1934, the year after Hitler came to power, through reports from Germany. To us this was just another such place. Nobody could have imagined that it was to be the largest and most murderous camp of all, the most horrible place that ever existed in the history of mankind.

Committee of the local youth organization. Freedom or "Dror". Upper row from Left to: Frumkah Dolnoroza, Kibbutz member, Hershl Springer, Kibbutz Chairman, Alizah, his girlfriend. Lower left: the author, Adek Greenwald, local youth activist, Frumkah Plotnitzkah, delegate from the movement in Warsaw, Gedalia Sobkowski, local trade union leader, Abram Fishel, local youth activist.

The head of the Jewish community in Auschwitz was a fine, educated man named Shenker. Because of his knowledge of German and his position in the community, he was able to get in touch with various Nazi and Gestapo leaders. An intelligent man, he had grasped the hopelessness of the Jewish situation very early.

The town of Auschwitz was only twenty miles from the Slovakian border. There was comparatively little persecution in Slovakia, which was a German satellite at the time. More important, however, was the fact that from Slovakia it was easy to get to Hungary, where one could feel safe. And from Hungary it was possible to get to Israel.

Mr. Shenker succeeded in bribing some Gestapo officers and borders guards, got together a group of children and sent them over to Slovakia. When he learned his plan had succeeded he did it again. Once again he had good news, coming from deep within Slovakia and Hungary.

Seeing that he had found a possible means of saving hundreds of people, Shenker got in touch with "Hechalutz" in Warsaw and offered his help. It was a great hope. Hechalutz immediately adopted the project and assigned it to Frumkah Plotnitzkah, a member of their Central Committee. She regularly undertook dangerous missions all over Poland, traveling under the false papers of a Polish Catholic, distributing literature, and keeping in contact with Jewish organizations throughout the country.

For some time, however, Mr. Shenker had been in the bad books of the Jewish dictator Merin. Merin did not yet know about the Slovakian venture, but he was jealous of Shenker's good relations with the Gestapo and angry that anyone but himself should dare to undertake such a connection. Looking for a way to get rid of Shenker, he finally found one as a result of the rescue scheme.

The few transports of children that had already reached Slovakia sent word that they were safe. A group of chalutzim now sent a similar message from the same place, and another such group from Warsaw was soon to form the next transport. It had to pass through Bendzin on the way and planned to rest there after the long and dangerous journey from the Polish capital. However, as the whole Slovakian project was top secret, no one in the community was to know about the group's destination. Not even the members of the youth organizations knew what was going on.

Now it happened that Molczadzki, chairman of the local Judenrat, paid the kibbutz one of his occasional visits. At that time he still enjoyed the group's full confidence, being considered someone who was trying to help save the community. No one suspected then that he had already sold his soul to Merin. So he sat talking with the kibbutz members, asking how the farm and the youth work were going and so forth. He was even shown copies of the youth bulletin. In the course of this conversation he urged the youth organizations to suspend their projects on the grounds that they weren't worth the risk involved.

This visit took place on the day the group arrived from Warsaw. Seeing people he didn't know, Molczadski went over to talk to them. They did not reveal their destination to him, but later Hershl Springer, the kibbutz leader, told him that these people were going to Slovakia by way of Auschwitz with the help of the community leaders there. At that time the kibbutz did not know about Merin's enmity toward Shenker.

Two days later the group continued on its way. A few days after that they came back and told us the end of the story.

When they arrived in Auschwitz they learned that the Gestapo was looking for Mr. Shenker and had arrested his family as hostages for him. The last transport of children had been stopped at the border and forced to come back. Mr. Shenker gave himself up to save his family and disappeared into the cellars of the Gestapo without a trace. The Warsaw group had to flee Auschwitz as quickly as possible. The kibbutz went into mourning. In those terrible times we grasped at any hope, however slight, but now we knew our hope had been in vain.

A few months later Frumkah Plotnitzkah told us that we ourselves were the ones responsible for the Slovakian tragedy. It had been learned in Auschwitz that Merin had told the Gestapo high command about the children's transport scheme and in this way had finally gotten rid of Shenker. Hershl Springer bitterly regretted telling Molczadski about the Slovakian maneuver. Who could have known then what a true servant of Merin's he was?

After the collapse of the Slovakian project about thirty of the comrades from Warsaw remained with the kibbutz. They soon found work, some in the laundry and others in town. It was less easy to get the local police to provide them with identity papers, but this was eventually accomplished by means of a bribe.

The presence of the new element revived the kibbutz's spirit. Frumkah was among them, and together they were able to re establish the true atmosphere of pioneering brotherhood. A few new chaverim (Hebrew for comrades) joined from the town, and the kibbutz, now numbering forty members, was once more able to exert a decisive influence on the town's youth.

Ideological Regroupments

The victory of the Red Army at Stalingrad had its impact on our little world in the Bendzin ghetto. The popularity of the leftwing organizations increased and many people joined them, while at the same time the rightwing groups lost a part of their membership. The Stalinist group in particular was strengthened, and the town's attitude in general became more pro Soviet. The Red Army was now regarded as our only possible saviour.

The local situation at this time was very bad, with thousands of people being taken away to the forced labor camps. There were also two so called "resettlements" of older people. We didn't know at the time exactly what this meant, although we knew enough to suspect they would never come back. Later we learned that they had been the first victims of the gas chambers. In all, the town had lost about ten thousand people up to this point. From the General Government came news of mass executions and exterminations by means of gas chambers, and now and then a survivor of some town that had been wiped out would succeed in getting to us. Into this situation came the news from Stalingrad, inspiring people with new life. The Communist paper gave details about huge German casualties, whole Nazi armies smashed. What a joy it was to read it. People began to hope again.

The best known and most active members of the Stalinist group in town were the young Bobo Graubard and another boy named Zabner, who was the son of a well known teacher at the Yavneh School. In the Trotskyite group the acknowledged leader was Aronek Ehrlich. (His brother, Sevek, had been a well known Trotskyite before the war.). These two Communists groups had to work in the strictest secrecy, but all the young people knew about each other's affiliations as a result of the heated discussion that went on continuously on the farm and in town.

One outstanding group was the leftwing youth of the Poale Zion, which included some unusually intelligent and scholarly people. Jacob Weizman, though a Yeshiva graduate, was an authority on Marxism and well informed on very many subjects. Ziml Krakauer, who was only nineteen, was so gifted in the study of philosophy that it was hard to keep up with him in a discussion.

The ideological realignments, which took place in the wake of the Russian victory, also affected the kibbutz. Its members began to debate such issues as who represented the working class in this war, and whether we should orient ourselves toward the Western powers or toward the Soviet Union. These discussions took up many long evening hours. One group believed that after Hitler was defeated the workers of Western Europe would take power and socialism would be realized there. Another, smaller group believed that the Soviet Union had to be the standard-bearer for socialism in Europe. The first group said, "We should consider Russia as nothing more than an ally and maintain a social democratic attitude toward her," while the second group was opposed to an alliance with the social democratic parties.

Frumkah later told us that the same discussions were going on at the Central Committee of the Hechalutz. Her own opinion on the matter was not entirely clear. Her first love was Israel and Zionism, and she had little faith in the possibility of socialism ever coming to the West. She was primarily concerned, not with what she would like to see happen, but with what she thought in fact would happen, and she summed up her conclusions thus: "The Soviet Union will not be defeated, nor will the Western democracies embrace socialism."

The discussions concerning Israel were marked by longing and despair. We knew that the Jews in Palestine were trying to save those in Europe, but we also knew that this was an impossible task, and none of us believed there would be enough Jewish pioneers to settle in the land of Israel when the war finally came to an end. We longed for news from Palestine and bitterly lamented our lost chances of going there.

Baruch Gaftek, a romantic type and a poet who later became the leader of our defense, wrote a song about Israel, which became very popular. Here is a verse in translation.

O you my land

I dream of you from afar
My hope in the depths of despair
Is you, my only land.

    Baruch was also an enthusiastic singer. Most of his songs were pessimistic. He wrote them while he was in a slave labor camp in Kleinmangersdorf, from which the kibbutz eventually rescued him. While there he won the respect and admiration of everyone around him. He was the foreman of a work gang consisting of fifty people, and his behavior was such that everyone in camp wanted to work under him. It was only while writing his poems, however, that he allowed himself to express the horror he felt at what he saw happening around him.

I
The world around me is constricted.
Doors and gates are closed
They are all locked,
They are all closed.

II
Thousands of clouds
Blow coldly
Toward the end of mankind
Toward the end of the world.

III
The whole world behind bars
One huge, dark prison
In the whole world only rulers and slaves
Convulsed in agony.

IV
With clouds of smoke the sky is gray
And with blood the earth is red.
Where is mankind, where is freedom?
It's no use, there is no sense.

This same man found the strength to stand as leader of the underground resistance until the very moment of his heroic death. A poet and fighter, he had also been the kibbutz's Hebrew teacher and a part of its very soul. His whole life was a lesson for all who came after him.

Political Parties

The activities of the Jewish political parties in our town were loosely organized at best, because of the lack of leadership. The original leaders were mostly in the Judenrat, which gave them a different point of view. They considered the work of their council the only activity that mattered. The parties they had led spent most of their efforts on financial assistance to members and on attempts to influence the council. However, as mentioned before, the left wing of the Poale-Zion remained firmly opposed to the Judenrat and its leaders. The party's right wing was quite active, especially in the matter of monetary aid to its members' families. Its leader, the unionist Gedaliah Sobkowski, was also opposed to the council. Relations between the two wings of the party were good, although their contacts were infrequent. The other Zionist parties were paralyzed because their leaders were all on the Judenrat.

We had no contact with any non Jewish parties, chiefly because we were afraid that there might be informers amongst them who would denounce us. In any case the Polish parties were not particularly active in Bendzin. There was only one Polish figure that kept up relations with the Jewish youth of the town. This was a professor in the local gymnasium named Mr. Stanek. He was well known as an athlete, since twice a day, morning and evening, he jogged through the streets of the town with his little dog. He was also an excellent swimmer, bathing in winter under the ice. However, few people knew, that he was also a scientific scholar and a socialist. Despite the possible consequences of doing so, he encouraged the young Jews of the town to visit him and borrow books from his library, which was particularly well endowed in the areas of science and social studies. Mr. Stanek sympathized deeply with the plight of the Jews. Several times he was offered the chance to become a Volksdeutsch (an honorary German who would be eligible for certain high privileges) but he refused. In a word, he was one of the very few true friends of our people on the outside. One day the Gestapo came, took him away to a slave labor camp (he was in his sixties) and destroyed his library.

CHAPTER IV- THE LAST PERIOD

August 12, 1942–August 1, 1943

The First Mass Extermination

Despite various instances of maltreatment and the deportation of a large part of the town's youth to slave labor camps, our political, cultural and educational activities continued relatively undisturbed. Yet the Germans had not ceased making themselves brutally felt in the life of the small, isolated Jewish community. On August 12, 1942, a tragic day for the whole province, all hopes that extermination might somehow be avoided were finally destroyed.

A few days before, the Gestapo had announced that the entire Jewish population was to report to two collection points on August 12 at five A.M. These two places were the stadiums of the HaKoah sports club and the Polish Sarmacia club. Similar orders were issued to the Jews of the other towns of the region, so that on that day the entire Jewish population of the province would be gathered together in five or six places. The announcement stated that all Jews had to be there, including the old, the sick, infants and pregnant women. Those not obeying the order would be deported to the east and their possessions confiscated.

I do not exaggerate when I say that the community was thrown into a panic. Even on the last day many people were still half crazy with the confusion of not knowing what to do. In order to deceive them, the Gestapo had staged a similar event the week before in the small town of Strzemieszyce. This had ended with a few people being sent to forced labor camps. The ruse did not succeed, however. It was obvious to everyone that the three main communities of the region were all being rounded up on the same day for some special reason. But there was no way to escape, we were in a cage. Molczadski, addressing the Judenrat, asked its members not only to obey the order fully but to urge others to do the same – otherwise he warned, they would be "running a risk." In return for their cooperation he promised to do everything possible to insure that the families of the council members would not suffer. The expression "running a risk" was one he always used when calling for obedience to the Nazis, and it was sarcastically repeated throughout the town.

The youth movements, unfortunately, had not taken a decisive stand on the roundup. Confused, the great majority of them went to the stadium. The officials of the Jewish Council said that in all probability nothing would happen outside of a few unemployed youngsters being sent to the labor camps. Almost all organization members had work cards that, they expected, would protect them and their families. Alas, they were mistaken.

Early on the morning of August 12 people began streaming along the main street to the two collecting points. (For this one day the Gestapo had revoked the order forbidding the use of the main streets to Jews, as these were the only routes to the stadiums.) The streets were clogged with people, including women with baby carriages and infants in their arms. Everyone carried their working papers, hoping these would save them. A few people who had no such papers hid instead of coming to the stadium.

The Jewish militia was already in the stadium when the crowd began arriving. A few SS men and some civilian officials of the Gestapo came a little later. By seven A.M. it was apparent that German soldiers were stationed at different points around the stadium with machine guns, watching the crowd. For those who began to regret that they had come, it was too late to escape.

At one P.M. the Gestapo officials began the selection process. They divided the soccer field into several parts, each separated from the others and guarded by the militia or the Gestapo. One part of the field was filled with the Jewish population. In the center stood the Gestapo or the SS beasts doing the work. Three long, narrow lines of guards stretched away from them, each leading to one of the three areas marked off in the remaining part of the field. Each person was driven along one of those lines to the area ordered for him, which represented his destiny.

The people sent to Field One were to be freed. Those in Field Two were sent to labor camps in Germany. Field Three meant deportation to Auschwitz, or death. In the Sarmacia stadium the selection was made by a brutal SS officer named Messinger; in the Hakoah stadium there was an animal in white gloves named Kutchinski. Jews accompanied by their families and holding their working papers, moved in a long line toward him, who stood in one spot waiting for them. Sometimes he didn't even look at the person or his papers before saying the number; one, two, or three. The rest was done by the local Jewish militia. They chased the person or family to the appointed place, goading them with sticks and clubs if they didn't move quickly enough.

In the Stadium

Some people sent to Field Three tried to save their lives by running in another direction but they were caught, beaten savagely and brought back. Field Three was large enough to contain all the people Kutchinski sent to it, who for the most part were families with more than one child. Parents with more than two children knew beforehand that they would be going to Auschwitz. Young children without parents also suffered this fate. Boys and girls without working papers went to Field Two. Only young people with work cards from important factories went to Field One.

For three days and three nights people stood waiting their turns, at times in the pouring rain. The SS men, after "working" for a few hours, took a rest or went to sleep drunk. At night it was cold and women with children suffered bitterly. Many lost consciousness, especially among the

The Last Jews of Bendzin

infants. Parents had not brought enough food as they had expected to be returning home the same day.

Plan of the Hakoach Stadium on August 12, 1942- Mass Deportation Day

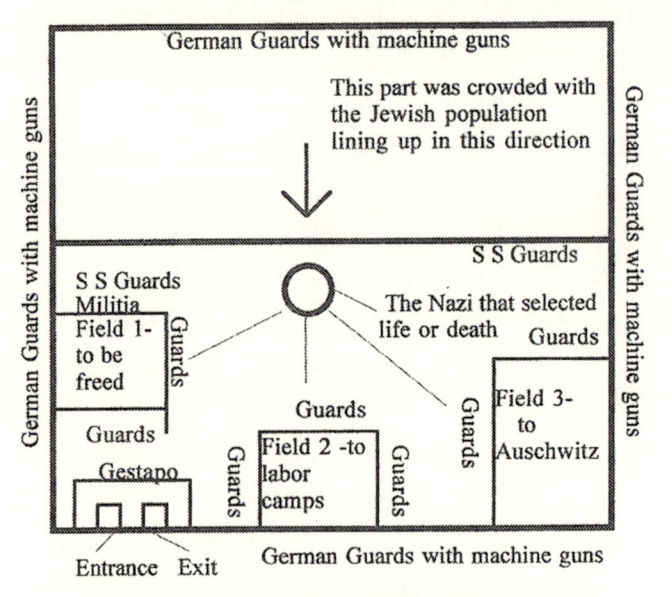

```
┌─────────────────────────────────────────────┐
│       German Guards with machine guns       │
│                                             │
│  G           This part was crowded with   G │
│  e           the Jewish population        e │
│  r           lining up in this direction  r │
│  m                     ↓                  m │
│  a                                        a │
│  n  ┌─────────────────────────────────┐   n │
│     │              S S Guards         │     │
│  G  │ S S Guards                      │  G  │
│  u  │ Militia      ○  The Nazi that   │  u  │
│  a  │ Field 1-        selected        │  a  │
│  r  │ to be      G    life or death   │  r  │
│  d  │ freed      u              Guards│  d  │
│  s  │            a                    │  s  │
│     │  Guards    r    G       Field 3-│     │
│  w  │            d    u       to      │  w  │
│  i  │  Gestapo   s  G a       Auschwitz│  i  │
│  t  │           ┌─┐ u r ┌───┐ ┌──────┐│  t  │
│  h  │           │ │ a d │F 2│ │      ││  h  │
│     │           └─┘ r s │lab│ │      ││     │
│  m  │              d    │cmp│ │      ││  m  │
│  g  │              s    └───┘ └──────┘│  g  │
│     └──┬─┬─┬────────────────────────────┘    │
│        │ │ │                                 │
│      Entrance Exit  German Guards with machine guns │
└─────────────────────────────────────────────┘
```

Plan of the Hakoach Stadium

The Nazi Kutchinski stood like a statue. (I heard that after the war he lived as a free man in West Germany.) He would point at his victim and scream one, two or three - very often, however, three. When people tried to show him working papers in an attempt to save their lives, he began beating them like a madman with his riding whip. The people he sent to Field Three amounted to about thirty percent of the total population. According to Kutchinski, the Nazis' principle in making selections was "humane, not to divide families." If there were a few people in a family who were able to work and one who was not, like an old father or mother, then the whole family went to Field Three. This had the tragic result that later families divided themselves up before going to the devilish beast in an attempt to save those of their members who were strong and healthy. Mothers left their children, sons and daughters their old fathers, or parents divided their children up and went to stand before the "judge" of life and death with only part of their families.

Terrible scenes took place. The weeping was horrible to hear as members of families said goodbye to each other forever. Some young people refused to leave their parents and went with them to Field Three.

After three days and nights in the stadium, the people from Field Three were taken to various buildings in town, there to be detained until trains were available to carry them east. The buildings used for this purpose were the orphanage, the market hall and the Agudat Israel School. The greatest numbers of people were sent to the orphanage, as it was large and located near the railway station. Previous transports had all left from there, the ones for the labor camps as well as the ones bound for Auschwitz. The Nazis had even remodeled the home for its new purpose by putting bars on the windows. Armed SS troopers guarded it during its use as a detention center.

Saving Lives

The young people of Bendzin did a great deal of rescue work during the roundups in the stadiums and in the days immediately following, when Jews were being detained in various buildings around town until trains were available to take them to Auschwitz. This delay in transportation enabled us to save hundreds of additional lives.

While still in the stadium we organized into "running groups" those children whose parents had abandoned them when they learned they could only survive if they had less than three children. There were also children from the orphanage. Together we gathered them into groups, telling them that at a certain signal they must start to run, breaking through the lines of SS guards. About twenty percent were forced back by the swinging clubs of the Jewish Militia and the gunfire of the guards, but most succeeded in getting through the lines to Field One, where they mingled with those chosen for freedom. Members of the youth organizations risked their lives by wearing fake armbands designed to resemble those of the auxiliary militia. Falling upon people in Field Three and pretending to beat and revile them, they kicked and drove them to a safer field.

Far greater rescue work was done in the temporary detention centers where people were awaiting transport to their deaths. Among these victims were children whom we wanted to save at any cost. It was dangerous work - one false step could mean disaster. The young members of the pioneer organizations decided that their first step would have to be getting positions inside the orphanage as kitchen workers or sanitation workers.

Once there, they had to smuggle people out of the various rooms in which they were being held. So, if a pot of coffee was brought to such a room, it was always brought by one person, but taken away by two - one holding each side of the pot. The guards at the door hardly noticed these changes since sometimes one person went up and sometimes two, and in any case the traffic and confusion were tremendous. Besides these distractions, the crying and weeping of the women and children were quite indescribable.

The men and women who were successfully smuggled out of their prison rooms were brought to the kitchen, where the next problem was how to get them out of the building. In the yard outside a German guard marched up and down, up and down. What to do? Our answer lay in the huge pile of refuse that leaned against the fence at one corner of the yard. While the German soldier was down at the other end of the yard, two or more people from the building would carry garbage pails out to this heap. One would climb it and jump over the fence to safety. Time after time, two or three people would make their way to the garbage heap in the back yard. Time after time, one less would come back.

A large number of orphans were saved by being taken away in the vans in which bakers brought bread to the detention centers. This was done with the knowledge of Chairman Molczadski, who had a special feeling for the children from the orphanage.

Together with a few other boys from the kibbutz, I worked in the Orphanage for three days and nights without sleep, wearing a false armband and carrying papers saying that I was in the Jewish Militia. The slightest suspicion on the part of the Gestapo as to what we were doing would have meant our immediate deaths. On the third night, while helping the mother of our young comrade Nathan Schweitzer to escape, I was caught by a German guard outside the orphanage. He made us both stand against the wall with our hands up and was about to shoot us when it suddenly occurred to him that there might be more like me. He looked over my papers, saw they were forged and began questioning me. My only answer was that I had found them. Since we were near the police precinct, he took us there, where I was again questioned. Again I replied by saying I had found the papers. Since they didn't consider it worth their while to bother further with a single Jewish man and woman, they sent us along with three others to the railroad station to await the train to Auschwitz. One of the three was Marcus Pohorille, a friend of mine from the kibbutz who had earlier tried to rescue his girlfriend's parents. When we reached the station, we discovered that it was too early and that the other members of the transport were still in the Orphanage. Being too lazy to wait, our guard decided to take us back there. Once there we thought we might have a chance to escape, and we did. There was no one on guard when we got back except one SS man who was always drunk, so we were saved.

Great bravery was shown by the young people who tried to rescue their fathers and mothers. The parents of Israel Groswald, a well known youth leader, were being held in the Judenrat Headquarters on Modrzjowska Street. The house was sealed on all sides and a police guard stood at the gate. Israel's parents had not come home from the stadium. They were old people and had been sent to Field Three. Now they were locked up in a room in this building, awaiting transport to Auschwitz.

Israel came home from the stadium to a silent, empty house and decided to do something. Taking some carpentry tools, he crossed over the roofs of the neighboring buildings to the headquarters of the Judenrat. It was midnight. He started breaking the bricks out of the wall, one after another, got into the building and led his parents out. Several other people escaped with them. Abraham Mendrowski was another I knew who displayed great courage. Before the war he had belonged to another kibbutz elsewhere in the country, but after the unsuccessful attempt to escape the Nazi invasion at the beginning of the war, he came to Kibbutz Borochov. His father was known in the old marketplace as Kive Schlosser (Kive the locksmith). Like many others, Abraham came home from the stadium without his parents. He knew where they were, however, and went there with tools from his father's shop. With the greatest care he began working on the wall, a fraction of an inch at a time. He ground away until he had made a hole in the wall about the size of a human head. Then he enlarged the opening, crawled through, and rescued his parents. Abraham later immigrated to Israel but, although he was able to save his parents that time, they were taken away in a subsequent transport. Many young men showed limitless courage, not all of them were successful. Those who were discovered joined the transport. In general, a large part of the rescue work was done by members of the youth organizations. They were particularly interested in saving more young people who would later be able to take part in the resistance.

Abraham Mendrowski with his family in Israel

On the third day of the prisoners' stay in the temporary quarters, the Gestapo forced the railroad company to deliver a train for the transport to Auschwitz. The chairman of the Judenrat, then still on friendly terms with us, told us a sad story. At a conference between the Gestapo and the railroad officials the latter explained that they had no trains to spare for the death transports, as they were all needed to take supplies to the eastern front. The Gestapo officer stood up and replied, "Then we will not send supplies to the front. But trains for taking the Jews to Auschwitz we must have." Thus did the will to exterminate override all other plans. The gas chambers at the death camp had probably stood idle for a day or two, and now the Moloch was hungry for more victims. Of course, trains were immediately provided and the transport went ahead as scheduled. At the last minute a thousand people were added to it from the nearby town of Dombrova.

It was later revealed that the director of the railroad had been bribed with a large sum of money and jewels by people trying for the longest possible delay in the hope that they would be able to rescue their relatives in the meantime. Alas.

About one tenth of all the people collected in the stadiums died there. From the rest, ten thousand were sent to Auschwitz and one thousand more to the slave labor camps. The result of the roundup in Sosnowitz was similar, and in Dombrova it was worse.

The Problem of Self Defense

After the roundup in the stadiums a deathly silence descended on the Jewish community, consisting of those remaining from Field One. The shock of having so many young people taken away stunned those who were left, and their minds could not work normally for a while after the unbearable tension of three days in the field. People sat at home and mourned friends and relatives who had been taken away in the transport. They also mourned any hopes they may have had of surviving the Nazi hell by leading a normal life.

Again and again we asked ourselves why the Nazis were doing this. We were not fighting against them as would enemy soldiers at the front, and even among the Germans' potential enemies we were not numerically significant. Why, then, were they murdering thousands of civilians? What were they getting out of it? There was no logical answer.

The town's whole cultural life had stopped; the schools, the libraries, the educational program, everything. No one even thought about these things now. They were meaningless in the face of what had happened. Yet life had to go on, even though the wounds were still open. The factories warned that people who failed to appear for work would have their ration cards taken away or would be deported. People began to return to their daily lives, whispering that perhaps the beast was now satisfied and would stop.

The first youth meetings held after the tragedy were quiet ones. Members asked one another what could possibly be done now. This question was deliberated by the Moazah and all the groups within it. Most of us believed the Nazis wanted to kill us all, regardless of whether we were able to work or not. This seemed obvious since the majority of people put on the transport had been able bodied. However many people in town disagreed with this. Their argument was that if the Nazis had wanted to kill us all, they could easily have done so in the stadium. Therefore, the rest of us were probably safe now. It was hard for the youth leadership to reach a decision. Who could have known then what the Nazis were planning? One thing alone seemed clear. We were in a prison, a cage, and escape was most likely impossible.

From the government, which the Nazis had set up over German occupied Poland, came terrible stories of whole towns wiped out by mass shootings. Even so, a large number of people in Bendzin still did not believe that the ultimate goal of the transports was the gas chamber or the oven. Orthodox Jewish circles went so far as to forbid discussion of the matter entirely. Meanwhile, in our own debates about the situation, two points of view gradually emerged. One was called Hatzalah, or Rescue; the other Haganah, or Self Defense.

The adherents of Hatzalah said there was nothing we could do against the Germans. Armed resistance would be useless since we were too weak and isolated, and moreover could expect no help from the Polish population. The only thing to do was to concentrate on rescuing individual

Jews by equipping them with false papers, which would enable them to go to Germany as Polish Catholic workers.

The adherents of Haganah said that the pioneering movement should be thinking of the safety of the whole community and not simply those individuals lucky enough to possess non Jewish faces. We were one with our people and it was our duty to be saved with them or die with them. If death was certain, we were to die in a way that would bring honor on ourselves both as human beings and as Jews. That meant setting up an armed resistance to the Germans with every means at our disposal and, when extermination was unavoidable, standing and fighting to the last.

Nearly all the youth groups agreed with the Haganah position. The only group opposed to this were the Trotzkyists. One wing of Gordonia urged the Hatzalah view on the grounds that armed resistance would mean certain destruction for the community. Whether they were right or wrong, this group was thinking first of all of Jewish survival. The Trotzkyists were another matter. They had evolved a strange Marxist theory. Invoking Lenin, they said that armed struggle only had meaning in a "revolutionary situation". Since this was a "reactionary situation", armed resistance would be worthless. Their duty now was to create propaganda, which would prepare the masses for another "revolutionary situation". How they extracted such an interpretation from Lenin no one ever knew. Even later, when we had been confined to a ghetto, these people still said they were an "international party" and could not take part in "merely" Jewish events. In their Polish language publication, The Red Flag, an article appeared entitled "What Not To Do." Regarding the Jewish situation it recommended sitting down and doing nothing, as anything that could be done would be senseless. This group had very little influence in town, however, since it was extremely small.

The youth groups began to reorganize. Only older teenagers were to be admitted from now on. Each organization was now divided into groups of five members, bound to strict secrecy. Overall administration was in the hands of the Moazah. Baruch Gaftek, twenty-seven years old, and a kibbutz member, was newly appointed to coordinate the work of the

The Last Jews of Bendzin

groups. He had had military training and was an exemplary pioneer. The Haganah's plan in case of further mass murder or deportation was to set fire to the town, maintain an armed resistance for as long as they could and then, if possible, to join the partisans. Unfortunately a few days later the entire Jewish population of the town was resettled in the suburb of Kamionka and the village of Srodula, where our farm was located. The Poles who had lived in these places were moved into the vacant Jewish apartments in town. Jews were forbidden to leave their new settlements and Gentiles were forbidden to enter, so that a ghetto was in effect created.

This new isolation of the community was considered a bad sign, although the council leader Merin assured us that we were safer now and should be more optimistic. Meanwhile the Haganah was trying to buy arms, but this proved impossible in our district. They did succeed in buying benzine, a necessity since gasoline was being rationed and no Jew had ration cards for it.

The Story of the Partisans

The Judenrat was aware of the plans under way for Jewish self defense and saw in them only a threat to its own safety. It ordered the Jewish militia to keep an eye on the members of the secret organizations, and the homes of such people were often searched. Merin made a speech in which he said that he would destroy anyone who attempted defensive action, arguing that such action would only bring further misfortune on the community. He promised to see to it that there would be no more mass murder, saying that the Gestapo had already promised him this. He called on the community to denounce anyone who continued to participate in illegal activity.

The first blow fell when the Communist group was wiped out. The arrests were made under Merin's personal supervision. They took place immediately after a certain Koslowski had been denounced for selling bonds in support of the Polish Peoples' Army, an underground organization under the influence of the illegal Communist Party. Koslowski was called before Merin for a hearing. What was said on that occasion was unknown, but house searches were already underway. The first person to be arrested was a woman named Gucia Lustig; a booklet of the Polish war bonds had been discovered in her house. On Merin's orders she was delivered to the Gestapo. She was tortured terribly and we later learned that they had cut her body with razor blades while interrogating her. The Gestapo's methods were well known and it was obvious to everyone that after a few more arrests they would have all the names they wanted. About ten people were arrested in all. A few succeeded in hiding. The destruction of the Communist group was like a thunderbolt. Young activists were deeply depressed to realize how difficult it would be to conceal anything from the Judenrat, who, it was now clear, had agents throughout the shops and factories.

A few weeks later the parents of the young men arrested received a letter from the Judenrat's central office, stating that the persons listed below had been sentenced to death by the Gestapo, and shot before a firing squad for high treason. The sentence was carried out on March 29, 1943, in Auschwitz.

On the list were the following persons:
1. Ber Graubart
2. Kalman Brodkiewitz
3. Naftali Braitbard
4. Chaim Jacobson
5. Aaron Merin (no relation of the head of the district Judenrat)
6. Wolf Sheinberg
7. Moshe Sheinberg
8. Samuel Leib Zacharias

(The photocopy of the original German document was shown to me by the father of Bobo [Ber] Graubert in Germany in 1947.)

Later the Gestapo arrested one of the men who had escaped, a youth named Lublink who was discovered hiding in a private apartment. Only one person had known of his hiding place, a certain Sobkowski (not to be confused with Gedaliah Sobkowski, the trade unionist and Poale Zion leader). It was believed that this was the man who had denounced the whole group to the Gestapo. The Gestapo then passed this information on to Merin, who made the actual arrests. Shpicberg, an official of the Judenrat of the time, who later immigrated to the United States, mentioned later that even the Judenrat wondered how Lublink had been found. Lublink had been the son of a well known and highly respected religious family, and the militia had not tried very hard to track him down. After he was arrested, Molczadski and Merin visited him in the cellar and asked who had betrayed him. He replied that only Sobkowski had known about his hiding place and that, moreover, only he had known about some money he had hidden in a coal box. When they arrested him, the Gestapo had told him to take the money out of the coal box. Furthermore, Szymek Gutman, an active Poale Zion member, later related a pertinent conversation he had had with Sobkowski's sister in Auschwitz in which she told him that her brother only denounced Communists. This creature survived the war and lived hidden in Bavaria.

As all attempts to buy arms had failed, some young men tried other methods. One of these, Harry Blumenfrucht of Hanoar Hatzioni, who had a somewhat gentile appearance, walked into the apartment of the SS man Michatz one day. Threatening those present with a fake gun, he forced them to hand over their real ones. Back on the street again, however, he was recognized by a German and seized. Hanged, he went to his death courageously. His parents were sent to Auschwitz, although his brother and sister escaped death in a labor camp.

The Haganah never did succeed in getting the arms it needed; a few old guns were all it had to train people with on the farm. The acquisition of sufficient weapons could have multiplied its strength many times over.

At about this time the Sosnowitz ghetto was closed and its inhabitants moved to Srodula Gorna (Upper Srodula), not far from where the Bendzin ghetto was located. The living conditions in this, our own prison, were terrible. Two or three families had to share a room, beds were stacked on top of each other. The inhabitants suffered from hunger as the ghetto was virtually cut off from the outside world. Gestapo men would come in from time to time and take away people they saw on the street. They never came back.

It was a desperate situation, with no arms and the possibility of new murders each day. Because of this we decided to join the partisans. Open resistance without guns could accomplish little, but hidden in the forests perhaps the young people could find an opportunity to fight the Nazis more effectively. They were ready to try, and so the first brave group was chosen.

Marek Folman, who was on the Central Committee of Dror, knew a Pole who was in contact with a group of partisans in the forest of Zawiercie. Acting as a guide, this Pole led our boys and girls out of the ghetto under cover of darkness one night. A few days later the guide came back with a scrap of paper saying that the group had reached a certain place and should proceed. Encouraged, a second group of ten of our best young people set out with the guide. A few more days passed with no word. Then one of the members of the second group, Ajzyk Newman of Hashomer Hatzair, returned to the ghetto and told us the terrible story. Exhausted to the point of death, he gasped, "They are all dead. The guide is a traitor." Ajzyk, then seventeen years old, told the story,

"We marched only at night. During the day we hid in the forest. The guide led us where people were not seen very often. We felt safer in the forest than on the road. All the time we were thinking how glad we would be to meet the partisans and get guns so that we could fight.

At midnight of the second day we sat down to eat something. We hadn't had anything to drink for two days and the guide said he would go to a village nearby for water. We didn't suspect anything. An hour passed and he didn't come back. Suddenly we heard footsteps and shouts of 'Hands up!' in German. We were taken by surprise and began to run but we soon saw they had us surrounded. They started to shoot us with machine guns.

Bullets came from all sides. Our people fell one after another. I looked around and saw that I was the only one left alive. I don't know where I got the idea, but I fell down and played dead. I lay face down without moving. They shot a few more rounds and then it was quiet. The Germans came nearer and looked at the dead bodies, laughing sadistically. With them was the Polish guide. He counted the bodies and said, "That's all of them. There were ten." They looked around and left. I lay for a half an hour without moving, afraid of a trap. Then I got up and came back the way we had gone. I went the rest of the night until I came to a road. Then I pretended to be a Polish boy until I got to the ghetto."

Ajzyk's listeners received his story with the silence of despair. They had hoped to be the first in our town to avenge their people. There were twenty of them and they represented six groups. Bachratz, Shmuel Finkelstein, Alter Goldbrum, Vovek Goldstein, Itzhak Kruvka, another Itzhak and Ziporah Marder were from the Kibbutz and Dror. David Kozlowski, Halah Katzengold, Lea and Idzia Pesachson and Moshe Urbach were from Hashomer Hatzair. And Gordonia gave us Abraham and Zalman Tenenberg, Israel Sheintel and Eljash Salo. There were also four more from Hanoar Hatzioni and Hashomer Hadati, but I was not able to get their names.

In the ghetto, morale went steadily down. Imprisonment was becoming harder and harder to bear. There was no outlet for our energy or our will to resist, and this drove us to desperation. We considered creating a partisan group of our own, but realized this would be impossible without the cooperation of the Polish population living near the forests. We couldn't count on that, rather the reverse. The only thing left to do was to wait and hope that somehow we could get guns.

At about this time the Haganah began to build camouflaged bunkers. These hiding places, most of them underground, were now our only means of escaping deportation. Naturally they were far from architecturally ideal as their builders had few of the necessary tools.

Meanwhile we lost one of the most active girls in the Haganah, Irkah Pesachson. The eighteen year old Irkah had gone to Warsaw to try to get arms, and we were counting heavily on her. She sent the Haganah a letter saying that she had gotten a bomb and was coming home. But she had no identification papers and was arrested on the train. We never heard from her again. Irkah belonged to Hashomer Hatzair and was the youngest of three sisters who were active in the resistance throughout the war. All three were magnificent idealists, ready to make any sacrifice for their people. Their father was a well known Bundist. Old Pesachson went to his transport with great dignity. Full of contempt for the Nazi who was pushing him on, he spat in his face, thus ending his own life.

The Collaborators Disappear

In June of 1943, a few days before the second expulsion of Jews from Bendzin, something extremely important happened. Gestapo officials came to the central office of the district Judenrat and called together its most important and influential members: Merin, Mrs. Czarna, Dr. Liberman, Dr. Loewenstein and Dr. Borenstein. These people were then put in a car and driven away to an unknown destination, and that was the last we ever heard of them.

Their disappearance came as a tremendous shock to us. The man in the street had believed that Merin's position with the Gestapo was assured, and that if any Jews at all were to be saved, he and his sycophants would be the ones. We could remember a Gestapo official announcing at a public meeting, when calling for obedience to the Judenrat, "Wenn der Merin bricht, bricht ihr alle" (When Merin goes, you all go). His downfall was therefore taken as proof that the end must be near.

Various rumors circulated as to why the Nazis had decided to liquidate their collaborators at this particular time. Some people claimed they had been eliminated because the Nazis feared they knew too much. Another theory, plausible though never proven, concerned the Paraguayan papers.

For some time now, certain people had been receiving immigration permits to Paraguay, which conferred automatic Paraguayan citizenship on their bearers. After the German law was passed ordering all foreign citizens to be interned within 24 hours, people with such papers were put into a special camp under the care of the International Red Cross.

We understood that conditions at this camp were relatively good, and so considered people who got into it to be rescued.

The Paraguayan papers were sent to us from Switzerland by the Hechalutz representative there, Nathan Schwalbe, who was now the only contact we had left with the outside world. Aware of the situation in our province, and informed that the foreigners' internment camps now represented the only possibility for rescue, he sent us a second batch of papers. Instructions came with them, directing the youth groups to decide who should be selected for rescue, and to send photographs of those chosen back to Switzerland.

Now Merin became aware of the importance of the work being done and saw how many people could be saved by it. Once again, he was furious at having been left out. Was it right that he, the dictator of the whole community, should have no say in deciding who was to be rescued? So he informed the youth groups that he too wanted to be among those who selected the recipients of the papers.

The organizations refused, whereupon he threatened to stop the operation entirely, and when the third batch of papers arrived he confiscated them. (He was able to do this because the local post office was under his control.) In due course, our friends in Switzerland learned that the third group of people had never arrived at the internment camp, and after that things moved quickly. The Paraguayan Consulate in Switzerland lodged a formal complaint at the German Embassy there, which in turn notified our local Gestapo leaders. They summoned Merin and demanded to know why he had kept the papers from being issued. At that point, one assumed, he had to tell them the whole story, and they could see for themselves his "disloyalty" in not telling them sooner.

In consequence, the next group of people selected to receive Paraguayan passports were rounded up and sent to Auschwitz. Dreier, the Nazi in charge of the district, tore up their papers with his own hands. Thus two things came to an end at once: the Paraguayan rescue scheme and the Central Upper Silesian Judenrat with Merin at its head.

Among those sent to Auschwitz were the eighteen year old Nadzia Klugman, a popular and brilliant member of Hashomer Hatzair; Leib Hollander, who was active in Dror; and Alex Statler, a leading member of Hanoar Hatzioni.

After the liquidation of the district council, the members of the local councils began to fear for their lives. The new Liaison man for the district, a former friend of Merin's named Smietana, tried to calm everyone down with a public proclamation ordering everyone to return to their daily routine and cooperate with the Germans. They needed us for work, he said, and would treat us fairly from now on.

The Second Expulsion

The ghetto of Bendzin was sealed shut in the middle of June 1943. A few days later, on June 22, at about 4A.M., formations of guards from the SS, the SA and the Gestapo surrounded the ghetto and entered it. Some families had night guards; they noticed the soldiers and alerted the people, whereupon those who had bunkers hid in them. The Germans went from house to house, driving out whatever people they found and beating those who didn't dress quickly enough. They spared no one, women or children, old or very young, and those who were unable to walk they shot on the spot. When they realized they had not collected as many people as they should have, they started looking for the bunkers.

During this expulsion the Nazis' final deception was revealed. Up until then they had assured us that people working in war plants would be spared. Yet now the SS men doing the selecting took whomever they wanted without showing any interest whatever in where their victims worked. Three to Auschwitz, one free: that was the ratio. About four thousand people were sent to the death camps that night, many of them young. They were taken directly to the gas chambers, as members of the "Canada" groups later told us. ("Canada" was the name given to those inmates of Auschwitz assigned to meeting the transports and taking them to the gas chamber.)

The great majority of people who did not hide failed to do so because Alfred Rosner, the German part owner of the most important factory in town, had told them that he had arranged with the Nazis that his workers were not to be touched. It should be mentioned that he was not guilty of this. The Germans had indeed made him that promise, and then broke it. Alfred Rosner was in fact a unique German who had saved Jews from danger many times, defying the Nazis when they wanted to take people away from his shop. It's true that he received "gifts" for his actions, running into the hundreds of thousands of marks, but he was worth it. His factory employed ten thousand people and was regarded as a last bastion of safety. Many times he had gone to Berlin to obtain a certificate stating that his factory was engaged in top priority war work. The Gestapo didn't like the fact that he intervened on behalf of Jews so often, and suspected that he was not a true Nazi. Finally one day they arrested him and kept him in jail for a while, trying to force him to confess his disloyalty. He never did, but they kept him locked up anyway, and a few weeks later we heard that he had killed himself in prison. (More likely, he was murdered by the Gestapo.) His shop workers mourned him, and those who knew him well assured us that he was, indeed, far from being a Nazi.

Another illusion which was destroyed during this second expulsion occurred when the Nazis took a number of officials from the local Judenrat off to their deaths along with the others. Until this happened we had believed such people would be the last to go. They believed it themselves, as did the members of the Jewish militia who were sometimes hardly less brutal than the Nazis. Yet now council members were being taken to the transport, and the militia who escorted them to the station were ordered to board the train as well and share their fate. From that day on the remaining council members ceased to look upon themselves as different from any other Jews. At last they understood that for the Germans one Jew was like another, the only difference between them being that some would die sooner and some later. Until now the Nazis had used false promises to get their victims to kill each other off; now their true colors were known to all. No longer did the Judenrat rush to obey their orders.

Inhumanity

The great majority of the Jews of Upper Silesia had now been killed in Auschwitz. Those left behind were now shut up in a ghetto outside of town. The Nazi soldiers no longer had to worry about the screams of dying women and children disturbing the afternoon mood of the soldiers who were quartered in town.

The Haganah lost many of its members during the second expulsion as a result of everyone's faith in the security afforded by the Rosner factory. Afterwards a few came back; they had managed to jump from moving trains. The chances of jumping safely were very low and nearly all who tried it were killed. A few SS soldiers traveled on the outside of each car and whenever someone jumped they would all fire on him at once. In addition, the person jumping would often break an arm or a leg in the process. One who came back was Hershl Springer, with a bullet in his foot; he had jumped just before the train reached Auschwitz. Others were Josef Rosensaft, later head of the Bergen Belsen Survivors Association; Jonah Schnol, of Hanoar Hatzioni; and Joel Springer, Hershl's brother. Ninety percent of those who jumped and made it were handed over to the Gestapo by the Poles as soon as they reached a human settlement. Many, many more young people could have survived if not for this fact. Very little Christianity was shown by our Polish neighbors at this time.

Meanwhile the inhabitants of the ghetto were paralyzed with the agony of waiting for the end. The council members lost their heads and all but stopped working completely. Like everyone else, they no longer looked for anything but a good bunker in which to hide.

The Haganah still existed in the sense that there were still people organized into groups, but it was completely unable to fulfill its function of self-defense as there were no arms to be had anywhere. To undertake resistance now would do nothing but hasten the final extermination. Those who persisted in "still hoping" would claim that the Haganah had shared in the guilt for the death of the community.

Hundreds of people sought to save their lives after the expulsion by volunteering for the labor camps. They bribed German officials or their intermediaries with their last valuables, hoping to be put on the trains

The Last Jews of Bendzin

to such places. The Germans pocketed the money and then, occasionally, diverted the trains to Auschwitz. But after a while even attempts such as these were impossible.

Only two ways of staying alive now remained to members of the Jewish community: the bunkers, or "Aryan" papers, certifying that the bearer was a Polish Catholic. These were very difficult to obtain. Some were stolen from Poles and some were smuggled in from the area under the General Government, but in the end very few people were able to get possession of them.

The situation was very slightly less bleak for girls, whose Jewish origin could not be proved conclusively even if they were caught without papers. So some girls in the Haganah decided to try their luck at escaping. Among them was Nitzah Bilard, whom I later married. Several children from the orphanage succeeded in getting into Germany as Polish Catholic orphans. The kibbutz members, Alizah Zitenfeld and Sarah Kukialka, who were in charge of them, lost their lives while trying to get them into Slovakia in early 1944. For most people the only hope left lay in a good bunker, and these began to grow in number. The Haganah had some, as did the kibbutz and the other youth groups. These had already saved some lives at the time of the second expulsion. Now literature was being written in them, calling upon the Jews who remained not to go to their deaths without resistance, but to sell their lives dearly.

Sarah Kukialka member of the kibbutz, active in "Saving Lives"

Frumkah Plotnitzkah, the spiritual leader of the remaining Jewish youth of Bendzin, lived in one of those bunkers. Wholly devoted to the Haganah, she had suffered much after the death of her sister Chantziah during the revolt of the Warsaw Ghetto, in which so many young fighters had died. There was a radio in her bunker, and using young boys as messengers she was able to communicate news from the outside world to the other bunkers.

The remnants of the youth were ready to fight to the end. If only someone could have given them guns and said, "Come, brothers, let us fight against the enemy and die." No one could say it, there were no guns - although there was now money to buy them if that had only been possible. A few days before the very end a German from Prague came to the ghetto and delivered fifty thousand marks to the kibbutz which, he said, came from Israel via Switzerland. Although there was no possible way we could have bought guns with it, the money nevertheless served as a symbol of the fact that our brothers and sisters in the land of Israel were thinking of us. Nor were they the only ones who donated money in those last days. People who had never wanted anything to do with the Haganah

The Last Jews of Bendzin

before now gave abundantly. It was all for nothing. The time when money could have saved us was long past.

The Last Days of Bendzin

On the night of August 1, 1943, the night guards noticed that German military and police units were surrounding the ghetto. Trucks were converging on the section from all sides, these contained German reinforcements from neighboring towns. There were also armored cars equipped with searchlights. When the patrols had completely encircled the ghetto, the Germans prepared for their great offensive on the helpless, broken, half starved village that was the Jewish settlement. Having been alerted by the Haganah, everyone tried to hide somewhere.

Exploding shells lit the ghetto as if it were noon. Cautiously, the Nazi gangs began to enter the ghetto one by one. They came in their steel helmets, with their machine guns and hand grenades at the ready. They had learned what had happened in Warsaw and were afraid that the same thing might happen here. Meanwhile the Haganah hid, huddled together, in the bunkers, hardly one of which had so much as a single gun.

The Germans began their murderous work, entering homes and driving out everyone they found, while their loudspeakers ordered all to show themselves. When these tactics did not yield a sufficient number of victims they began to search with German thoroughness behind walls and in attics and cellars. When they discovered a bunker they killed its inhabitants. They shot the old, and the sick. They raged through apartments smashing furniture, beds, and mirrors. They were in their element. At the collection point they set up in the center of the ghetto, they began torturing people in an effort to learn where the bunkers were. Hardly anyone told them. One man pointed out a few and lost his mind a short while later.

Meanwhile conditions in the bunkers were growing steadily worse. Most did not have enough water or food. Communication between them was only possible at night, when the Nazis stopped their work to watch the darkness being torn apart by rockets and mortars. Whenever they noticed any movement, a whole battery of machine guns would open up on the spot. Nevertheless messengers, mostly the youngest boys and girls from the kibbutz or any orphans the kibbutz had saved, still crept from bunker to bunker during the intervals of darkness, hearing news. Sad news: two more bunkers were discovered that day, a hundred more people shot. The living could hardly gather the dead each night. And a group of people was set apart, earmarked for transport to Auschwitz.

But all this was not enough to satisfy the Nazis. Comparing the number of people they had taken with the number of ration cards that had been issued, they concluded that some people had still escaped them. After searching for three days they found a Haganah bunker, the main one. They began firing on it and yelling, "Juden heraus!" (Jews get out!) Suddenly, from inside the bunker, two guns opened fire and two of the SS thugs fell bleeding to the ground. The SS gang retreated and shot again. Again the two guns answered them. The Nazis brought machine guns and threw in hand grenades. The bunker burst into flames but the gunfire from inside continued. Finally, after an hour, no further sign of life came from the bunker, but the Nazis still did not dare to enter it and instead ordered their fire brigade to drown it.

It had been Frumkah's bunker. With her were Baruch Gaftek, Frumke Dolnoruzah, Tziporah Botzian, Hedvah Bernard, Tovia Dvorski and Peninah Jakubovitz. These heroes and heroines had all been members of Kibbutz Borochov.

The inhabitants of another Haganah bunker, not yet discovered, had by this time gone for four days without water or air and were reaching the end of their endurance. Mr. Boehm, the local Judenrat's new liaison man, who had a sentimental feeling for the pioneer movement, tried to save them by bribing a German policeman to take them out of the bunker and put them in the work gang which the Germans had set up to clear the bodies. As soon as they came out of the bunker the police handed them over to the Gestapo. Zvi Brandes, a leading member of Hashomer Hatzair, tried to run away when he saw this but was shot. Hershl Springer, trying the same thing, met the same fate.

At the farm a desperate fight was going on. The members of a few different organizations had managed to get some guns and had barricaded themselves in the dormitory, where they fought a last pitched battle with the Nazis. Soon, however, the wooden building caught fire and they had to flee. They tried to fight their way through the Nazi lines, but this was impossible, and they were outnumbered ten to one by machine gunning soldiers. They died heroes.

At the end of seven days the ghetto of Bendzin was no more. Fifteen hundred people lay dead in the streets. Those who were left alive were sent to Auschwitz. Here and there a bunker still remained undiscovered, the people in those crept out of the ghetto and took refuge in another dugout in the Polish section, near the old Jewish cemetery. A few individuals succeeded in getting to Hungary and from there to Israel. A few more joined the gang put to work gathering clothing, linen, silver and sewing machines by the SS. These spoils were later sent to Germany and the gang to a concentration camp. The ghetto then stood empty.

EPILOGUE

At the same time that Bendzin's Jewish community was meeting its ultimate fate, the same thing was happening in the ghetto of Sosnowitz and several other small places where Jews were still living as factory laborers.

Auschwitz survivors who had worked at the gas chambers told us that when the transports from Bendzin came in, there was one train the Nazis never unloaded. Instead, they opened its doors and then emptied their machine guns into it, killing everyone inside. This they did because the train had been mutinous on the way, with more than the usual number of people jumping off. One of the SS guards had even been killed. The troopers were afraid such people might make one last desperate show of resistance before the gas chambers, a spectacle the Germans were eager to avoid. So ended nine hundred years of Jewish history in the town of Bendzin.

CHAPTER V – SILHOUETTES

Baruch Gaftek

  Baruch Gaftek was his full name but we all called him Baruch. Everyone in town admired and respected him. In part they were won over by his pleasant voice, his dark curly hair and black eyes, but they also saw the beauty of his spirit.

  He had been born in Pultusk and had graduated from the Hebrew Teachers' Seminary in Warsaw, which was not far. He wanted to go to Israel, and Hechalutz accordingly sent him to Kibbutz Borochov for a brief period of preparation. He arrived just two months before the war began. During the unsuccessful attempt to escape from the Nazis at the very beginning of the war, he was caught with some others at a bridge over the Warta River, near Olkusz. The Germans drowned many people in the river, but Baruch was able to swim to safety, coming home with a lung infection.

  At the end of 1940 he was sent to a labor camp, where by the strength of his character he was able to create a small island of humanity and brotherhood in a world of darkness and savagery. But his health declined steadily, and the kibbutz succeeded in bringing him back. When he left he took the blessings of everyone in the camp with him.

  He was among the first to organize a self defense unit and was subsequently made leader of the Haganah. In 1934 he had attended a school for military instructors and strategists set up by the Hechalutz, now he had an awesome responsibility. The smile left his face. After the failure of the partisan scheme there was nothing to do but await the final extermination. In order to ease the burden of this terrible knowledge, he wrote. His few free moments he spent with the girl he deeply loved.

At the end he devoted himself to the work of the Haganah twenty-four hours a day. The one thing he was unable to do in spite of his most frantic efforts was to get weapons for the fighters. When the last days came he was filled with bitterness at the thought that his hands would be empty. But at last, at the very end, he got his wish; his was the bunker with the two guns. He died knowing that a murderer had fallen by his hand. When it was all over and they took the bodies out, his hand still gripped its gun in a spasm, defiant beyond death.

Hershl Springer

Hershl came from Lodz, where he had been brought up in the slum section called Balut. A hundred thousand Jews lived there, jammed together in the worst poverty imaginable. Hershl's parents had been Labor Zionists, and he himself had been an active member of the youth movement Freiheit from his earliest years, eventually becoming one of its leaders. He also studied painting. In 1937 he was sent for "Hachsharah" (training) to Bendzin's Kibbutz Borochov, of which he eventually became treasurer. When emigration across the San River to the Russian sector began and Hechalutz's Central Board wanted the Bendzin kibbutz not to be entirely liquidated, Hershl remained in town. He worked in a factory as a night guard in order to be able to give his days to the role the kibbutz had assigned to him, that of liaison among the various youth organizations. Because of this job he was generally regarded as the spokesman for all the youth of the town, and indeed he was. It was thanks to his initiative that the farm was created, thereby providing an opportunity for pioneer training for hundreds of young people. Even the Judenrat listened when he talked, as they knew he represented the next generation. They wanted to have at least some good marks on their record for the time when the war would be over.

When the brutality of the Jewish militia went too far even for the members of the Jewish Council, they asked the Kibbutz to form a new militia. Hershl refused, even though he knew it meant a degree of security for the young people. He knew what liars the Judenrat members were and was disgusted at having to talk to them, but he had no choice since the kibbutz laundry worked for the community and was officially the property of the council.

Hershl, who had made his way back to town from a death transport with a bullet in his leg, was later in the bunker earmarked for transport to a labor camp, because of a bribe. However when the Germans emptied the bunker, they were enraged to find a radio and a gun hidden there, and turned the people over to the Gestapo instead. It was while Hershl was trying to escape that he was shot again, for the second and last time.

He stands before me now as I write, that good Hershl Springer who loved sentimental ballads and sang them with such gusto. He devoted his life, body and soul, to the work of the Hechalutz and the salvation of his people. He lived for the dream of Eretz Israel, where, some day when the war was over, he hoped to settle as a member of Kibbutz Hame'uchad.

Hanka Borenstein

A dark beauty, slender, with calm round black eyes, she had a soft voice and a silent way of moving. She was a Hebrew scholar, specializing in Tanach. She came from a cultured family. Her father was a professor in the Gymnasium and her mother an educated woman. By the time she was seventeen, Hanka knew Hebrew, Latin, Greek, German and French. She was a member of Gordonia and had been among the first to resume work in it after the war began. She was a tireless teacher in the children's school. Respected for her learning and character, she was unfortunately too frail physically to bear the strain of the work that fell to her in the later months. We often wished desperately we could get her abroad somehow.

She went to her death in one of the last transports, shortly before the end of the ghetto. She died in Auschwitz, and remains alive in the hearts of those who survived.

Nadzia Klugman

She was a pretty, blonde, energetic girl who moved and spoke with decisiveness. She was a good friend of Hanka Borenstein, although they were different in many ways, among them the fact that Nadzia was a member of Hashomer Hatzair. People often commented on how close they were in spite of their different ideas.

Nadzia came from a home where life was hard. There were three small children besides her, her father often had trouble finding work and her mother was sick. Nadzia supported her family with the money she earned giving lessons. Early on she had become one of the most active workers in her organization, and was one of the leaders of the children's school. After spending each day teaching, she would study. She read books on philosophy and sociology until late at night.

She put the movement above everything else. She had wanted to join the partisans but an accident had kept her out of that venture, thus saving her life. Later, she was chosen for a Paraguayan passport at the moment that the Gestapo got wind of the affair, and she was sent to Auschwitz.

I can see her now, hurrying along the street from one class to the next, her head bent in concentration, completely oblivious to the world around her.

Israel Diamant

"Israel is coming," somebody would say, and everyone immediately burst out laughing. When Israel talked, no matter what he was saying, he could make people laugh until the tears came.

It was after work hours on the farm. Everyone was lying around on the grass relaxing while Israel held forth. After each sentence he uttered, people would explode into fresh laughter. Hours passed, but no one wanted to leave his company.

Israel was among the leaders of Hanoar Hatzioni. Together with Carola Baum, who immigrated to Israel, he had restored this large busy organization to its full status after the war began. He was the merriest, liveliest boy in it. He worked on the farm, where he had the job of organizing the labor force and deciding who did what. It took all his skill to fulfill the requirements of the farm's economy and keep everyone satisfied at the same time. Later on, when he was in the Haganah, his work was doubled.

He also represented Hanoar Hatzioni on the Moazah, where he differed vehemently with the General Zionists who claimed to represent the movement on the Judenrat. He agreed with Korzuch, the Hanoar leader in Sosnowitz, in opposing Merin's policy of cooperating with the Gestapo in the matter of delivering people for Auschwitz.

There were disagreements among the many people with whom Israel worked, of course. But harmony united them in the end, and he had a major share in creating this.

Jacob Weizman

Jacob was the son of a very religious family. His brother had gone through Yeshiva and become a rabbi, and he himself had studied in a Yeshiva until the outbreak of the war.

Then he began to read world literature, as well as secular Jewish works. He soon arrived at a sympathetic understanding of Marxism. But he didn't stop there, he continued studying until he discovered the work of Borochov, which gave him a proper understanding of the Jewish question. He then joined the Borochov Youth, a leftwing group of Poale Zion.

None of this was easy for him. His parents noticed the change in him soon enough and it angered them, since he had promised them he would be a rabbi when he grew up. But nothing could hold him back. Because of his fantastic mind, he soon mastered idealist philosophy as well as dialectical materialism, and became the accepted philosophical authority around town. He puzzled people, although nothing ever puzzled him for long. Although he was invincible in an argument, he was never afraid to admit defeat if he saw that his opponent was in the right.

When the time for armed resistance came, he ceased to be a philosopher and became an activist. He collected bottles of benzine, fake militia uniforms, etc., and hid them near his home. Jacob left in the last transport. His bunker had had no guns.

He was unforgettable. It seems to me that I see him now, blinking for a moment over some difficult philosophical problem, then smiling as he begins to unravel its complexities for his listeners.

The Pesachson Sisters

They came from an outstanding family and represented three splendid types of workers and fighters.

Leah and Irkah had belonged to Hashomer Hatzair from earliest childhood, Idzia, who had been a socialist Bundist, joined her sisters' group at the beginning of the war. Their father, a prominent Bundist, had been a veteran of the Revolution of 1905. Not one to impose his ideas on others, he let his daughters make up their own minds on all political issues. In their turn they were scrupulously critical in every intellectual decision they made. In Hashomer Hatzair they formed a small, harmonious unit.

Leah spent a great deal of time at the kibbutz, where she enjoyed the atmosphere. The children loved her and she was like a mother to them.

Joining the movement meant a great deal to Idzia. She talked about it wherever she went. Whenever she met any of her old friends from the Bund she tried to impress upon them the importance of joining the resistance. She dreamed of dying with a gun in her hand. Together with Leah, she went to join the partisans. Both were happy that at last they were going to get their greatest wish.

The third and youngest was Irkah, who was a friend of Nadzia Klugman. They often worked together and in time took over the main work of Hashomer Hatzair. It was a great responsibility for them. Like

Nadziah, Irkah was blonde and didn't look Jewish to the super barbarians. Dressed like a Polish country girl, she traveled all over the country, going to Warsaw for journals and newspapers. It was from there that she brought us our first gun. Had she been caught while doing so, she would have been finished. She was happiest on Saturdays, when she could be with her organizational family. She would sit up with them far into the night, discussing plans and hopes.

Soon enough came the days of terror and murder. The Haganah was trying desperately to get arms, but all attempts failed. Then Irkah had an idea -Warsaw. Perhaps we could get something there. She applied for the mission and was accepted. Once again she set out for the capital, her life in danger every minute. She reached her destination and got a hold of a homemade bomb. Maybe the Haganah would be able to figure out how to reproduce it. Soon she was on her way back home. Everything went well, most of the way was covered. In another hour she would arrive in Bendzin. All at once a search of the train was announced. There was no time for her to hide. The policeman was screaming for everyone's identification papers. Irkah had no papers, only a bomb. She had to open her suitcase. When we learned that she had been caught, no one was able to speak.

She often told us stories about her journeys; how she mingled with the girls of the countryside, imitating their dialect, which differed from the Polish spoken in town, about how she smuggled forbidden literature under the very eyes of the Germans.

No one is left from this heroic family. All perished in the struggle.

Bobo Graubard

He was a young boy, Bobo. Those who did not know him well could not guess at the spirit and courage hidden behind the spectacles he wore.

Bobo came from an intelligent family and had been well educated. He had been a member of Hanoar Hatzioni from an early age, eventually becoming the head of a group as a result of his unusual intelligence. During the ideological realignments after Stalingrad, he moved to Hashomer Hatzair with a group of friends, but he didn't stop there. After a while he left Zionism entirely and joined the Communists. Only with them, he believed, could he fight fascism effectively.

In daily life, however, Bobo kept up his friendly relations with the pioneering youth and spent much of his time on the farm. We knew by the end of 1942 that a Communist youth group had been created and it was no secret to us that Bobo was active in it. Sometimes he would exchange publications with his friends in other organizations, and often he would try to win them over to his views. Later on we saw less of him, and it was generally assumed that he had been given more important work to do. It was more dangerous to belong to the Communists than to any other youth group. Selling bonds for the Polish army of liberation was particularly risky - too many people were afraid of Merin. The first bonds sold were brought to the Judenrat, and the arrests of the Communist group followed from that.

Bobo was the last of the group to be arrested, and it was in his hands whether any further arrests would be made. Although the youngest of the whole group, his character was such that he bore the inhuman tortures of the Gestapo without cracking. His parents tried frantically to rescue him, but to no avail. The Gestapo did let his father see him when they were finally finished with him. His face bearing the marks of his ordeal, he said, "I'm glad I didn't talk."

Frumkah Plotnitzkah

Bendzin had the good fortune to be visited by most of the leading members of the Jewish resistance in Poland. Of these, Frumkah was the first to arrive and the last to leave. She will remain forever in the memory of those who survived as the symbol of the fighting spirit of Warsaw and the Hechalutz.

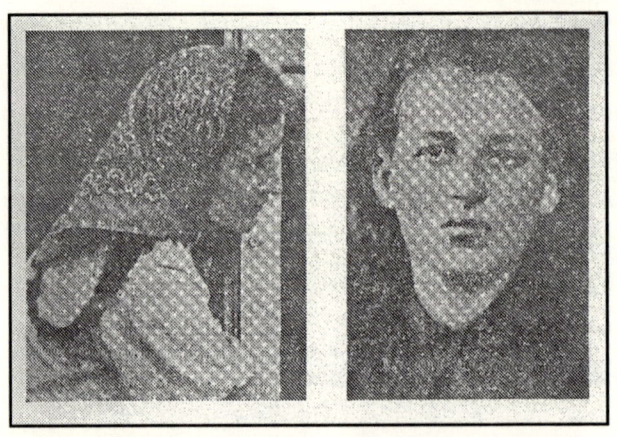

The two heroine sisters of the anti-Nazi movement in Poland: Chantziah and Frumkah Plotnizkah

She came to us for the first time a few days after the kibbutz returned to town, after the unsuccessful attempt to outdistance the Nazi invasion. She had been traveling around Poland, trying to find out what remained of the kibbutzim, and among those she visited was Kibbutz Borochov. Later on we had Tosia Altman, of Hashomer Hatzair, Leah Perlstein, leader of the kibbutz in Lodz, and Eliezer Geller, the head of Gordonia and one of the leaders of the Warsaw Ghetto revolt. Mordechai Anilewicz, the leader of the Warsaw uprising, came to us too and tried in vain to dissuade Merin from his obedience to the Gestapo. He tried to explain to the Judenrat leader that acquiescence to the Germans could accomplish nothing, since they were firmly committed to the extermination of the whole Jewish people. He wanted Merin to change his policy to one of resistance and rescue.

Chantziah Plotnitzkah, Frumkah's sister, came to us a few times. She was one of the bravest girls in the whole Zionist movement in Poland, traveling around the country like the wind on forged papers. Another who did this was Marek Folman, of the Central Committee of Dror.

These, the best and bravest of our generation, visited Bendzin. They came to a heartfelt welcome. They stayed long enough to point out the way for further struggle and then they left, going back once again to their dangerous posts in the outside world.

Frumkah came from Pinsk in eastern Poland. When she came to us for the first time she was twenty-five. Later on, when the Hechalutz ordered her to stay with us, our kibbutz was beginning to disintegrate. The frustration of training for Zionist socialism in Israel when it had become obvious that we would never get there was unbearable. Into this situation Frumkah came. She spoke to us simply and quietly, showing such understanding, such delicacy of feeling, that even those who disagreed with her most angrily became spiritually committed once again. People began to come to her with their problems. They always felt better after talking to her. Soon she was the general confidante. Life was just better when she was around, there was something in her that gave people new strength.

She had her troubles too. Her health was poor. Before the war she had been at Kibbutz Baranovitz, where food was scarce and work was hard. In addition to this, she was burdened by her terrible understanding of what was going on. No one understood so well as she the true nature and extent of the tragedy, and no one felt it so keenly. On her travels she had seen dozens of Poland's towns emptied of their Jews, she had seen Lodz, Warsaw, Krakow and many more. And then she learned that her only sister, Chantzia, had been killed while trying to escape from the Warsaw Ghetto in order to come to us.

We felt powerless to ease her suffering, even though it is true that the moments she spent with her comrades in the kibbutz were the only times she could forget her sorrows for a little while. The light would come back into her eyes when she discussed the literature of modern Israel, or explained the difficult philosophy of Shymonowitz' poem "The Matzeyva" (the monument).

Young and old loved her. Everyone knew that hers was one mouth that spoke only the truth. Yet Frumkah hadn't the heart to tell the truth she knew. Long before it was all over she had seen the whole picture, knew what the end would be - the end of a thousand years of Jewish culture and of three and a half million Jews.

Other Works by John Ranz

Tears on Tisha B'Av: Memoirs From the Holocaust

1929

I remember my childhood years at the home of my parents in the small yet famous city of Alexandrov, Poland. Jews made up one third of the twelve thousand inhabitants, and the city was known as the home of one of the largest Chasidic dynasties in Poland, which had members and admirers throughout the country.

In the late 1920's, my father, a secular Jew, rarely visited the local synagogue. When he did it was not to pray or participate in the ritual but simply to appease my grandparents on both sides. They feared that he would break away from the traditions of centuries. To allay their fears he would accompany them from time to time, taking my younger brother and me along.

One of these occasions was a mourning day in the religion, Tisha B'Av, which commemorated the day of the destruction of the Second Temple in Jerusalem and with it Jewish sovereignty. During the prayer, while I held my father's hand, I noticed that he was in a very serious mood, more so than his usual serious demeanor. We came to the chapter expressing grief over the loss of Jewish independence in the war with the Romans. Thus began the misfortunes and tragedies of the Jewish people. This event led to the exodus of the Jews from Israel and to life in the Diaspora.

Suddenly I noticed that my father had tears in his eyes. I had never seen my father cry before. I was shocked and frightened. This man of great courage, had come home, bloodied and injured, from fighting with Polish anti-Semitic hooligans who had assaulted the less resistant Chasidim. He was determined to show the Jew-haters that they would have to pay a price for molesting Jews. He was a hero in my eyes. Yet here he was, leaning against the wall, without a prayer book, covering his eyes so that I should not see his tears. He was reacting to the cantor's rendition of the Aicho chapter in the prayer book, which laments the defeat of the Jews by the Romans. I pulled at his sleeve, and asked, "Daddy, why are you crying?" I received no answer. This tragic melody has remained with me my entire life, as a result of the fright I experienced at seeing my hero-father's tears.

1941

Twelve years later, in 1941, in Nazi-occupied Poland, I was away from home at a training kibbutz of my youth movement in Upper Silesia. There we prepared for the pioneering life in Palestine. Because of the Nazi invasion of Poland we were no longer able to go there.

About fifty young men and women came together for an illegal meeting devoted to Tisha B'Av. We were in a serious, sad mood, our eyes downcast, sensing the catastrophic days looming ahead. One of our senior comrades observed, "German Fascism wants to annihilate us. Thousands of Jews have already been murdered. Who knows what terrible days await us if the war doesn't end soon?" Baruch Gaftek, an intellectual, who later died while fighting in the resistance, spoke these words. He concluded, "The history of the Jews in the Diaspora is one long chain of pogroms. In the 12th century there were the Crusades, in the 15th century the Inquisition and the expulsion from Spain, in the 17th century the Chmielnitski pogroms in the Ukraine, and in 1905 pogroms organized by the decaying Tsarist regime. In 1917-18 Petlura led the Ukrainian White Guards in a pogrom against the Jews, and now what awaits us?"

We read from Chaim Nachman Bialik, our great national poet's famous poem, City of Slaughter, where he describes the pogrom of

Inhumanity

Kishinev, Ukraine in 1903. Sitting there I recalled Tisha B'Av twelve years earlier with my father at the synagogue. Now I understood my father's tears. He was well versed in our people's history. He cried for the many Jews killed in the various pogroms. Now it became clear to me why this proud man, chosen by Alexandrov's Jewish community to organize and lead the defense against the Polish government inspired pogroms, cried.

1942

Tisha B'Av, 1942. I was in Bendzin Poland, a few days before the deportation of two thousand Jews. The Nazis chose mostly the very old and the very young. The poor souls were held in a special building where they waited for the trains to take them away. I had been assigned to infiltrate this building. With my forged identity papers, I posed as a member of the Judenrat (Jewish Council appointed by the Nazis to execute their orders) and was thus able to enter the building. My task was to rescue youngsters whom the resistance considered fit. The Gestapo inside and out guarded the building. The Jewish militia, obeying Nazi orders, was also guarding inside to prevent people from leaving their rooms. At first it seemed an impossible task. Later I found a way to bring out some of the youngsters. I chose the late night hours, when most of the guards were sleeping or relaxing, to operate. The rooms had no toilet facilities. Women and their children were lying on the floor and occasionally water was bought up from the kitchen downstairs. Posing as a kitchen helper I went up and down the stairs observing the various halls and choosing which youngsters I would help over the fence after midnight.

In one of the halls I saw men standing and praying. Intrigued, I approached them. I noticed that they were not reciting the usual daily prayers. I heard a heartbreaking lament in their voices. "What kind of prayer is this?" I asked. "Today is Tisha B'Av" they answered. I stood there for a moment, speechless. Their praying ended with most of them in tears. I choked down my own tears, and ran out of the room.

1943-45

During the next two years I encountered Tisha B'Av under different circumstances. In concentration camps there was no time or energy for sentiments and tears, only the daily struggle to survive. Life would often hang on a split second decision. The sole aim was to survive until the next day.

1946

It is now the summer of 1946, one year after the defeat of the Nazis by the combined strength of the Allies in the east and west. I had survived Buchenwald concentration camp by sheer luck and stubborn resistance. The luck mostly consisted of being helped by the prisoner underground, led by a coalition of leftist groups.

I am in the U.S. zone in the city of Regensburg, which is located in Bavaria, Germany. I work as a co-editor of a Jewish weekly serving the survivors living in the surrounding Displaced Persons' camps or in the cities of Bavaria. Each one of us waits impatiently for papers to immigrate, mostly to Palestine, or if they have relatives to other countries. The few survivors in Regensburg would meet together at the community center. One day I heard from them a familiar chant, a lament, and I realized that it must be Tisha B'Av. I tried to fight back tears; perhaps it was time to forget. The war was over, but deep inside it was not over. My mind recalled the last few years. The somber evening meeting at the Kibbutz with Bialik's angry, thundering verses, the scenes of deportation to Auschwitz from the ghetto, cries of mothers torn from their children, the shootings of innocent civilians, and the entire gamut of the Holocaust. My memory reached further back to my parents and grandparents. Again I saw my father in the synagogue covering his face so I should not see his tears.

I joined with the other survivors in commemorating the holiday, and thought about the causes of the tragedy of Jewish history. In this strange land of Germany, soaked with our blood and suffering, I contemplated. How long will this chain of tragedies continue? Will this ever change?

Will the world ever become more rational and will ethnic hatred and racism ever disappear?

> Summer, 1946
> Regensburg, Germany

Misconceptions and Truth About The Holocaust

By John Ranz

Only when we draw conclusions from the past can there be hope for the future.
Bertrand Russell

The Jewish community and the survivors of the Nazi Holocaust get together annually to commemorate the Holocaust and the end of Nazism - mankind's twelve year long nightmare.

It seems to me that in the years following the Holocaust wild grass has grown over the true story and subsequently the comprehension of the Holocaust has been distorted. A superficial or false approach is being circulated and expounded on this most important event of our people.

The memorial meetings have settled themselves into a routine, hardly relevant to the true facts of this event. After an outlet is given to our pain and outrage for all the injustices done to our people and after we honor the memory of the dead, we must ask ourselves, "How did it happen?" It is our moral obligation to get to the truth of the matter. Who are the ones responsible for the Holocaust, which social forces or economic classes brought it about? Eleven million people: six million Jews and five million non-Jews were murdered in concentration camps and ghettoes. They were gassed, burned, and starved. Entire populations were exterminated including women and children. It is to date the largest mass murder in the history of mankind.

Unfortunately, with rare exceptions, I have yet to witness a memorial meeting that addresses itself to this essential question. Is it ignorance or intentional avoidance of an insight into the true realm of the Holocaust? A superficial or incorrect treatment is a disservice to our legacy, to those we left behind in the ghettoes and concentration camps and to those who died fighting in the anti-Nazi resistance. And what about future generations? Don't we owe them an honest, truthful insight into the Holocaust?

Unfortunately, year after year, the memorial meetings continue to evade or distort the true causes of the Holocaust and its meaning.

For example, at some memorial meetings, one may hear the often-repeated "Amalek" theory. This identifies the German people with Amalek, who appear in the Bible as the eternal and most dangerous enemy of the Jewish people. They claim through mystical theories that Germans actually are the descendants of the Amalekites. That's theory number one. Another theory, that I heard in religious circles claims that we must have sinned by straying from the laws of the Torah and that the Holocaust is truly God's punishment. Otherwise, they claim, the Holocaust could not have happened. A third theory which speakers in anger often cite is a simple and primitive one. It is that the German people are a nation of murderers, a nation with a killer instinct. This killer instinct is sometimes dormant, sometimes awake.

I have listened to a noted scholar and Jewish philosopher, Professor Emil Fackenheim of Canada. This is a man of vast knowledge on the topic, yet I came away shattered and disappointed. His talk was mainly a dialogue with God, he was cautioning us humans not to judge God harshly, since we are not able to understand this awful, monstrous event. "Don't ask how God could allow these things to happen, we have no answer." He veiled the Holocaust in mysterious thoughts and advised against trying to comprehend the phenomenon. The closest he came to any assessment of human responsibility was in blaming all of Christianity, its saints not merely its sinners, for paving the way for the Holocaust. I claim that the above interpretations of the causes of the Holocaust are misleading and certainly cannot help us to prevent another one.

I propose that it is necessary to analyze the social, economic and historical conditions of Germany in the 1930's, in order to truly understand recent history. The Jewish tragedy and the events of World War II cost Europe forty million lives. Let us begin with Germany after World War 1. It lost the war and was stripped of its colonies and possessions. The economy was in disarray. The 1929 world crisis hit Germany hard and its economy continued to worsen. The working classes and the millions of unemployed were becoming desperate and many of them radicalized. There was a huge cry for bread and work. The masses, through their worker's parties, threatened to take over the country by winning the elections and curbing the privileges of the rich. The ruling classes became frightened and panicked. The arms and steel manufacturers and the bankers could not provide work or bread for millions of unemployed. The only way out of the crisis, the industrialists decided, was to enter the path of war and conquer new markets. In order to do so, a strong army was needed. The opposition of Socialists, Communists and labor unions had to be destroyed. The country had to be unified and geared to a war economy. The big German industrialists saw in the small nationalist anti-Marxist Nazi party a convenient vehicle for realizing their aims. Its vicious anti-Semitism, which gave a racial meaning to the deeply rooted Christian anti-Semitism, preached by the Nazi party, was just right.

The industrialists, and the Nazi propaganda they financed, blamed the Jews and used them as a scapegoat for Germany's ills. With the help of many millions of marks the industrialists and financiers supported and built Hitler's power. They had to make a choice. It was either their own power or privileges or the life of the Jews and the workers' parties. Hitler would never have been able to come to power without the support of the steel and arms manufacturers, known today as the military-industrial complex. With their money for propaganda it wasn't difficult to organize millions of unemployed and the impoverished middle class to rally around the nationalist slogans; Honor and fatherland, Germany needs Lebensraum, The War was never lost, corrupt generals betrayed us, or Gross Deutschland must be restored. It was easy to convince these millions that Jewish influence in Germany was out of proportion and must be eliminated.

The Nazi race theory of higher and lower races, of superhuman and subhuman, appealed to many Germans who were flattered at belonging to the pure Aryan race. This was but a secondary element in the Nazis rise to power. It is interesting that after the Nazis achieved their highest electoral victory in January 1932 with 13,700,000 votes, in the next election in June 1932 they had a defeat, and obtained 11,700,000, a loss of two million votes. Their popularity was declining. Just at this moment the bankers and financiers, fearful that Hitler would not gain power through democratic means, decided to take matters into their own hands.

On January 4, 1933 a meeting between the top forty German industrialists and Foreign Minister Von Papen, Hitler, Himmler and Hess, took place in Cologne, Germany. The meeting was at the home of Kurt von Schrader, of Bank Schrader, who represented the banking industry. At the close of the meeting von Papen emerged beaming and declared jubilantly, "Gentlemen we have just concluded an agreement with Mr. Hitler." At this moment the foundations for the ensuing war and the Holocaust were laid. It is with these people that the historical responsibility for the war and the millions of innocents murdered by the Nazis rests. Without their financial support the ensuing tragedy would have been impossible. They held the key and handed it to Hitler. They agreed to all of Hitler's proposals. Such was the testimony of Schrader at the Nuremburg trial on July 21, 1947. Hitler's proposals consisted of eliminating the Jews from all walks of life, smashing the labor parties, the trade unions, and dissolving all the other liberal parties.

Nazism as Seen by Its Non-Jewish Victims

The irrationality of the various interpretations mentioned earlier; God's punishment, Germany as Amalek, the German nation possessing a killer instinct, is particularly obvious when we consider the sizeable number of non-Jewish inmates in the concentration camps. Can these specifically

Jewish interpretations apply to French resistance fighters, to German Social Democrats, and to the Dutch, Belgian, Czech and other antifascists who were incarcerated in the camps? For these victims of Nazism anything but an analysis of the political and economic conditions in Germany would appear irrational. They were the first victims of the destruction of German democracy and Germany's rearming for a new war. First the Communist Party was smashed, their parliamentary representatives murdered. The next to share their fate were the Social Democrats, then the labor unions, and then a small number of clergymen who opposed Nazism. Ninety-five percent of the clergy in Germany cooperated with the Nazis.

In retrospect, the great historical mistake of all these forces, liberal and left of center was their inability to unite and form an anti-fascist block. It is impossible to be sure that had such a unified anti-fascist opposition been created it would have the changed the course of history. But certainly it is now clear that nothing would have been lost by such an effort. The consequences of not doing this proved to be a hundred times worse.

It deserves mentioning that the small group of German survivors of concentration camps, who barely make a living today in West Germany, see these former Nazi supporters: the Krupps, the Flicks, and the same bankers living in unbelievable prosperity. They have resumed their positions of power whereas the survivors are ignored. While a German survivor of Buchenwald, who courageously opposed Hitler and survived through a miracle, receives a meager pension of $150 per month, former Nazi officials get fat pensions of five or ten times as much. The whole judicial system was left almost unchanged, which explains the ridiculously light sentences for the mass killers, e.g. for the killing of five to ten thousand people-two to five years in prison, that is if their doctors don't object that they are unable to serve it for health reasons. This is however, another topic, which should be called "The Post-Holocaust Tragedy".

Christian Theology, How Much of a Factor?

A serious endeavor has been made to explain the cause of the Holocaust as a result of the Christian deicide dogma, or the claim of Jewish culpability in the death of Jesus. The Holocaust, it is said, was the result of two thousand years of accumulated hatred, which needed an outlet like an erupting volcano.

While nobody will deny that Christianity kept religious anti-Semitism alive for centuries and that it was a powerful tool, it was not the fundamental reason for the Holocaust. This type of anti-Semitism could have gone on for many more centuries. It wasn't the hatred on the part of the clergy that caused the Holocaust although it did clear the way for it, and made it palatable to the anti-Semites. Religious anti-Semitism exists in many countries. The deicide story continues in spite of the Pope's recent denunciation of it. The masses of Christians are still trapped in their own theory about Jesus being rejected by the Jews and will have much difficulty finding a way out.

Yet pogroms, let alone the Holocaust, were not caused by purely religious reasons. They came as a result of economic tension and the struggle for material goods and privileges. The pogroms and persecutions of the Jews in Poland before World War 1I were a result of the search for a scapegoat by the Polish semi-fascist ruling circles. Before the war Poland was involved in a deep class conflict. On one hand the small rich elite, on the other hand the millions of hungry peasants and workers who cried for bread and work. The situation became so desperate that the privileged classes had to find a scapegoat both to save their own skin and to cover their crimes against their people. Anti-Semitism became the official policy of the Polish government before the war and pogroms were becoming legal. The ruling classes, in order to protect their economical political power, used anti-Semitic sentiments nurtured by the church to incite the masses to violence and pogroms. A similar situation existed in Romania and other East European countries prior to the war.

Role of the Leaders of the Survivors in the Comprehension of Holocaust

The roots of our misconceptions of the Holocaust, particularly among survivors, stem from their not having been politically informed or active before the war. Many of today's survivors were children at the beginning of the Holocaust and the vast majority of them didn't have the time to analyze why there was a war, or a Hitler, or who was responsible for the Holocaust. They were too occupied building a new life and trying to be financially solvent, and some were very successful. Criticism of the dominant privileged classes of Germany in 1929-33 seems to the survivors a criticism and an indictment of the present privileged classes in the United States. That is taboo, a fear that can be explained as a form of disloyalty to the United States.

Most leaders of the survivor groups ignore the essentials of the Holocaust because it serves their financial interests. They are "nouveau riche". The leaders are well aware of who is historically guilty in the Holocaust but this is ignored since it conflicts with their present political interests, formed as they became more financially successful. It is actually a betrayal of the Holocaust legacy.

Instead of the Holocaust shaping their thinking and their political views, it is the reverse. Immediate political interests are altering their comprehension of the Holocaust and distorting its lesson. That is why memorial meetings almost never mention the causes of the Holocaust and why they are unable to draw conclusions for preventing another one. The annual gatherings are limited to the history of the brutality and extermination; to cries of anguish and suffering inflicted upon us by the Nazi-murderers. But the murderers weren't only the SS men or soldiers who personally killed or gassed. They were the Krupps, the Fricks, the Schraders, the von Papens who are equally guilty for planning the war and handing the state power to the Nazis. They have never paid for their crimes. They are as wealthy and as powerful today as ever. Who said crime does not pay? Not to examine the true causes and not to unmask the masterminds of the crime is a disservice to our people, even if it's not fashionable today, and not to the taste of some of our leaders.

How Can We Prevent a Holocaust?

Can we really? Let us boldly examine each option. Armed resistance? Can a small minority find security in armed resistance surrounded by a sea of enemies? Can an organized armed minority lacking support of the surrounding population defeat the military force of a modern state? Not a chance! All they can achieve is a heroic death. The Warsaw ghetto and other uprisings will forever be shining examples for future generations on how to die if we must die, but it is not a model of how to prevent a Holocaust. "What about Israel?" is often asked. The Holocaust certainly influenced the founding of the State, made clear its necessity, particularly in view of the passivity of the world around us. Israel must be defended with all our might as long as its enemies do not agree to allow it to live in peace. If the majority of Jews settled in Israel that might be a solution. Also Israel is able to take in Jews discriminated and expelled from other countries. But it does look as if Jews will remain in the Diaspora for the foreseeable future and so we are still vulnerable and exposed to danger. Argentina was a classical example of a country being torn apart by class conflicts. Argentina has half a million Jews, most of them in the middle class and in a most vulnerable condition. Anti-Semitism is virulent in the armed forces and in the police departments. Should the privileged classes, industrialists and large landowners decide that their position is critical they will divert the attention of the poor, landless masses from their inability to govern, to the Jews "who have everything". Jewish stores can freely be seen in main streets of Buenos-Aires. Where then lies safety or relative safety for us Jews from another Holocaust? I think that we must get involved wherever we live to influence life and society in such a way as to prevent a need for a scapegoat. We must struggle for an economic and political structure that has relative stability in order to avoid a situation where large masses of unemployed and desperate become prey and can be skillfully exploited by the privileged classes to save their own position of power. It is the privileged classes that abandon their social responsibility and cause class confrontation, fascism and war, but it was we who paid for their crimes.

Deep Economic Crises in Any Society with a Jewish Minority are Danger Signals

Confrontations between classes are also Holocaust danger signals. It is our duty to be alert to detect the symptoms of these danger signals and to do everything possible to work with and help those forces in society that are interested in change---changes toward economic stability and away from economic chaos, leading to a restructuring of our social order. True safety from another Holocaust lies in the creation of a society where tolerance, a humanitarian approach and human dignity are deeply ingrained. The basic prerequisite for such a reality is a proper economic climate; a base upon which human relations can grow and develop. A different and economically restructured society would improve human bonds and also weaken the religious Christian obsession with deicide. Only through changes in this direction lie possibilities for the prevention of new Holocausts and for eliminating them forever..

Printed in the United States
215700BV00001B/15/A